'Now here's a provocative idea. ... the frustration, disappointment, ev... ;ns of God's Spirit yearning within t... ags Duggan thinks so. Coming to us... n, wise from her wounds and sens... invitations from Jesus to find deeper grace and joy.'

Sheridan Voysey, writer, speaker and author

'Mags Duggan's wonderful new book is spiritual writing at its best. It's seriously rooted in the text of scripture; it suggests ways of applying the biblical narratives to our own contemporary and sometimes rather messy lives; and it points us inexorably to look to Jesus for transforming truth and grace. I can't recommend it enough! Read it and discover for yourself faith, joy, love and confidence in Jesus.'

Michael Parsons, pastor, editor and author of *How to Read the Bible* (BRF, 2020)

'Mags' unique gift of writing is evident in the way she uses scripture to speak into our heartfelt experiences. With authenticity, wisdom, sensitivity and gentle challenge, she invites us into deeper insights of what it is like to be fallible humans, yet dearly beloved children of our Father.'

Dr Pauline Yong, counsellor and spiritual director

'I found this a very moving book. Mags' honesty, insight and ability to cut through the pretence of Christian faith are profoundly helpful... Any thoughtful reader will be greatly blessed by this book as it will help them to find greater joy in the "better song" of Jesus Christ.'

Revd Canon Jonathan Perkin, vicar of St Andrews and St Bartholomew, Churchdown, Gloucester

'Mags' book draws us to a place of longing to respond to the invitations of Jesus. Whether it's responding to his invitation to fullness of life, to leave our past ways of thinking and enter his life-giving grace, to meet our deepest needs and desires, to rest in him, trust him or settle our home in his love, Mags shows us that there is hope for living a life transformed by Jesus.'

Karla Hawthorne, The Navigators, International Missionary Staff Care

'Mags has the ability to write words which can be read with ease and yet contain deep truths. As she explores some of the invitations of Jesus, she marries up theological and biblical references with personal examples which bring the truths of God to our own lives. As Mags points out, the central issue for any of the invitations from Jesus can be summarised as "Will you trust me?". Read the book to find out why it's so important that we do that.'

Sarah Hay, HR Manager European Christian Mission and Course Leader, Redcliffe College

The Bible Reading Fellowship
15 The Chambers, Vineyard
Abingdon OX14 3FE
brf.org.uk

The Bible Reading Fellowship (BRF) is a Registered Charity (233280)

ISBN 978 0 85746 876 5
First published 2020
10 9 8 7 6 5 4 3 2 1 0
All rights reserved

Text © Mags Duggan 2020
This edition © The Bible Reading Fellowship 2020
Cover image by Rebecca J Hall

The author asserts the moral right to be identified as the author of this work

Acknowledgements

Unless otherwise acknowledged, scripture quotations are from the Holy Bible, New Living Translation, copyright © 1996, 2004, 2007, 2013. Used by permission of Tyndale House Publishers, Inc., Carol Stream, Illinois 60188. All rights reserved. Scripture quotations marked with an abbreviation are taken from the version shown. All italics in these quotations are my own, except for quotes from AMP and AMPC. AMP: Amplified® Bible (AMP), Copyright © 2015 by The Lockman Foundation. Used by permission. www.Lockman.org. AMPC: Amplified® Bible, Classic Edition, Copyright © 1954, 1958, 1962, 1964, 1965, 1987 by The Lockman Foundation. Used by permission. www.Lockman.org. ESV: Holy Bible, English Standard Version, published by HarperCollins Publishers, © 2001 Crossway Bibles, a division of Good News Publishers. Used by permission. All rights reserved. JBP: The New Testament in Modern English by J.B. Phillips copyright © 1960, 1972 J.B. Phillips. Administered by The Archbishops' Council of the Church of England. Used by Permission. KJV: Authorised Version of the Bible (The King James Bible), the rights in which are vested in the Crown, are reproduced by permission of the Crown's Patentee, Cambridge University Press. MSG: The Message, copyright © 1993, 1994, 1995, 1996, 2000, 2001, 2002 by Eugene H. Peterson. Used by permission of NavPress. All rights reserved. Represented by Tyndale House Publishers, Inc. NCV: New Century Version®. Copyright © 2005 by Thomas Nelson. Used by permission. All rights reserved. NIV: The Holy Bible, New International Version (Anglicised edition) copyright © 1979, 1984, 2011 by Biblica. Used by permission of Hodder & Stoughton Publishers, a Hachette UK company. All rights reserved. 'NIV' is a registered trademark of Biblica. UK trademark number 1448790. NKJV: New King James Version®. Copyright © 1982 by Thomas Nelson. Used by permission. All rights reserved. NLV: New Life Version, copyright © 1969 and 2003. Used by permission of Barbour Publishing, Inc., Uhrichsville, Ohio 44683. All rights reserved. RSV: The Revised Standard Version of the Bible, copyright © 1946, 1952, 1971 by the Division of Christian Education of the National Council of the Churches of Christ in the United States of America. Used by permission. All rights reserved. TLB: The Living Bible copyright © 1971 by Tyndale House Foundation. Used by permission of Tyndale House Publishers Inc., Carol Stream, Illinois 60188. All rights reserved. TLV: Tree of Life Version Translation of the Bible. Copyright © 2015 by The Messianic Jewish Family Bible Society. TPT: The Passion Translation®. Copyright © 2017 by BroadStreet Publishing® Group, LLC. Used by permission. All rights reserved. thePassionTranslation.com

Every effort has been made to trace and contact copyright owners for material used in this resource. We apologise for any inadvertent omissions or errors, and would ask those concerned to contact us so that full acknowledgement can be made in the future.

A catalogue record for this book is available from the British Library

Printed and bound by CPI Group (UK) Ltd, Croydon CR0 4YY

A *better song* to *sing*

Finding life again through the invitations of Jesus

Mags Duggan

Foreword by **Tracy Cotterell**

In memory of Libby Hinton and Ruth Myers

Contents

Acknowledgements

This book actually began life about 15 years ago when I gave a series of talks on 'The invitations of Jesus' to a group of very weary missionaries from Central Asia who had gathered together for a break in Thailand. They needed to hear again that there was life beyond the fatigue, disappointments and demands that they were experiencing daily in their lives in those far-flung places they called home. The content of the book grew a little more in substance through retreats with ECM (European Christian Mission) workers and with UK Navigator staff, and then, finally, during another retreat at Penhurst Retreat Centre, it was suggested that I might want to put the content of the retreats into written form. Thank you to all who participated in those retreats and especially to those who encouraged me to put down on paper what was already written on my heart; your encouragement blessed this book into being.

There have been others whose encouragement has meant so much to me over the months spent writing the words which make up this book. The words 'Thank you' hardly seem adequate for the load of gratitude they carry, but they are meant with all my heart, so…

Thanks to Mike Parsons, friend and former editor, who was the first to see the notes which eventually became this book and liked what he saw. You somehow saw beyond the thin layer of those initial words to the substance beneath them. There would be no book without your wise eyes and generous heart. Thank you.

My thanks to all the team at BRF who have worked so hard in so many different ways to see the book released into the world.

Particular thanks to Olivia Warburton and Rachel Tranter, steady-handed, cool-headed, warm-hearted editors, whose encouragement and quiet enthusiasm have been such a support. Thank you for all the ways you've watched over my words with such skill, such care.

Special thanks, too, to Rebecca J Hall, whose stunning cover design was more than I could ever have hoped for. You heard my heart – and painted what you heard. Thank you for such a gift.

Most days, the act of writing is a joy and a sheer delight, but there are other days when it feels lonely and scary and I wonder if what I'm writing will make any sense to anyone, and that's when I've so needed support and prayer – and received it. So thanks to the men and women in Dave and Tracey's Connect group from St Andrew's, Churchdown; to near and dear friends Pauline, Rosemary, Shelley, Di, Diane, Ros, Tony, Ruth and Rich, Tzuchien and Amy, Anne and David, Jonathan and Jessica. Thanks to far away but near-in-heart friends Dave and Karen, Craig and Kris, Ed and Conni, John and Jen, Les and Karla, MaryKate, Karen K. Thank you for all the hours of listening that you have given me, for cups of coffee and (sometimes) cake, for holding me in prayer, for holding me in love, for lifting me up on to the shoulders of your confidence in God for me and for this book.

I hardly know how to express my thanks to Tracy Cotterell for such a beautifully written foreword. Thank you, Tracy, for so obviously understanding the intent of the book and for recognising the desire of my heart that all who read the book would discover a better song to sing in their own lives. Thank you for capturing all of that and for expressing it so richly and so warmly.

And finally, thanks to Karen Anderson, friend, listener, cheerleader and unofficial editor whose great gift to me was to read every word of every draft of every chapter with fresh eyes, a wise mind and a kind heart. Thank you for such a gift, and for the gift of your consistent encouragement and support and trust in God for me as I wrote; this book – and my life – is richer because of those gifts.

Foreword

Imagine a friend – a really good friend: someone you trust to handle the truths you're prepared to reveal to them about the secret disappointments, the unresolved restlessness, the yearnings for a richer, deeper, hope-filled life that's worth living as a follower of Jesus in your world.

Mags is such a friend – to me and to many others whom she's loved and encouraged and challenged over decades. She's also a skilled spiritual director, a sought-after speaker, a voracious reader, a faith-filled woman of prayer, a lover of beauty, a stunning singer and a generous host who manages to make every meal something of a feast, despite her reluctance to hang around too long in the kitchen.

There are some people you just want to spend time with because they have the godly gift of helping you see life afresh – your life, your context, your hopes and your fears. All of us have seasons when someone like that can make all the difference in the world. All of us, at times, find ourselves in a place we didn't choose, didn't hope for, doing things we didn't dream about or pray for. All of us, in an honest moment, might voice a disappointment or doubt in the God we've sought to know and to serve, or a dissatisfaction with ourselves as a disciple of Christ.

Though she laughs easily, Mags hasn't led an easy life, neither professionally nor personally. Nor has she shied away from people in pain, or confusion, or doubt, or faithlessness, or those who struggle to make sense of Jesus' invitation to abundant life right now. She's traversed the terrain of life-changing tragedy herself; she's lived through losses that have come in different forms over the years; she's walked through the wilderness.

But she has lived well.

She's lived well because she's lived honestly before God. She's lived well because her yearning to trust him deeply for a life worth living hasn't abated after all these years. She's lived well because she's lived in the real world – the disruptive world of jobs, and family, and finances, and organisations, and friends – and in the real and radical world of the Bible.

In all the ups and down, she's sought the life of Christ.

When is it a good time to write a book like this? When you've lived life over a long time and have come to trust the wisdom that you're offering to others. When you've walked closely enough with many different people and seen them come alive afresh to God. When you've ascended the mountains of joy and plumbed the depths of despair and today sing a better song than you sang all those years ago.

Mags has much wisdom to share about this life in Christ. In this book, she's chosen to explore just six of the many invitations Jesus extends to us. I guess she'd say they've been some of the great life-changing invitations for her, the ones she's wrestled with most.

Jesus' invitation to...

- abundant life in our real, everyday lives;
- freedom from beliefs and behaviours that bind us;
- refreshment through his thirst-quenching presence;
- vulnerability through naming our deepest desires and truest longings;
- rest from life-sapping burdens;
- peace by receiving his lavish love, offered with all wisdom and understanding.

Imagine a friend: a woman who would walk with you as you explore Jesus' invitations for yourself – in your world, in real life, with honesty and hope. If you've picked up this book, perhaps you're looking for such a friend. Read this book that way, for it has been written that way: written in prayer that you, the reader, would discover a better song to sing – in all of life, in your life. May it be so.

Tracy Cotterell
Managing Director, London Institute of Contemporary Christianity

Introduction

The film was totally engaging. Julie Walters, heartbreakingly convincing as Rita, a young working-class hairdresser who, in an effort to 'better herself', had enrolled in an Open University English literature course. Her assigned tutor was the initially uninterested, consistently drunk and divorce-threatened Dr Frank Bryant, played by Michael Caine. Through her course and her relationship with Dr Bryant, Rita was exposed to a world that was radically different from the one she had spent a lifetime living. The changes she experienced as she became more involved with the realities of this new life were challenging and not necessarily for the better, but in the midst of these changes, the rituals of the weekend remained the same. Most Saturday nights saw Rita and her husband, her sister and her sister's fiancé, her mum and her dad in the same pub they'd always gone to, sitting in the same seats they'd always sat in, drinking the same drinks they'd always drank, listening to the same music they'd always listened to. It was on one of these nights out, while everyone was singing along with uninhibited gusto to a song from the jukebox, that Rita turned her head for a moment and glanced at her mother, sitting, quiet, in the midst of the noise, clutching her drink, the tears on her cheeks wet and unwiped.

'What's wrong, Mother? Why are you crying?'

Her mother's response was simple and profound:

'There's got to be better songs to sing than this.'

That one line, just ten words long, perfectly summarised the plot of *Educating Rita* and Rita's own longing for a better song to sing. Sitting in the darkness of the cinema that night, on the surprised edge of my own tears, I felt a deep resonance with those words; I understood something of the weight of resigned disappointment they held.

I had been a Christian for about 15 years by then. Looking from the outside, I doubt anyone would have guessed how I was really feeling about my life; I had become very adept at mask-wearing in certain company. No one could have guessed the dimensions of my own disappointment – or the bewildering dissonance I was experiencing between what I had been taught and believed about how life should be as a follower of Jesus and the actual reality of my life. It felt like a lonely place to be in. I seemed to have picked up an unwritten rule that the voice which rose from within and shouted, 'Look, the emperor's got no clothes!' should be shushed, perhaps by prayer and a more rigorous commitment to a disciplined life. I'm not sure that works, but I am sure I'm not alone in the experience of disappointment and dissonance.

After many years of working as a counsellor and pastor, the American writer Stephen W. Smith observed that many sincere followers of Jesus are living wholesome lives of quiet desperation.[1] Perhaps his words describe where we are right now; perhaps the words uttered by Rita's mum clothe the growing ache and emptiness that we may have been feeling for a while, as we realise that the 'highs' of inspiring conferences and occasional retreats and the spiritual buzz of men's breakfasts or women's days have led to diminishing returns. The heart-soaring worship and the preaching we hear in our thriving church on a Sunday morning may move us for moments, sometimes even days, with the hope of a different way of living, but then it all fades and we are back to 'normal'. As time goes by, there seem to be fewer and fewer places that hold out the possibility of a richer, deeper, God-infused life. For many of us, such a life seems more dream than reality anyway. Richard Foster describes aspects of that dream graphically:

> Perhaps somewhere in the subterranean chambers of your life
> you have heard the call to deeper, fuller living. You have become
> weary of frothy experiences and shallow teaching. Every now
> and then you have caught glimpses, hints of something more
> than you have known.[2]

In over 30 years as a companion to men and women on their faith
journey with God, I have listened to many sincere followers of Jesus
as they've shared with me how worn out, bored, disappointed
and frustrated they feel about the life they are living – and how
ashamed and guilty they are for feeling this way. In quiet, sighing
moments of unmasked honesty, they may admit, 'There has to be
a better life to live than this – because *this* is no longer enough;
there has to be more.' But having made such a costly admission –
where to go? Perhaps better to just stuff that admission down into
the deepest pocket of our hearts – pushing it in among the dreams
and longings and hopes that are already gathering fluff there – and
get on with life; any other way holds the potential for even more
disappointment.

I wonder if these yearnings for 'more' in our experience of life as
a follower of Jesus are actually a deep-heart responsiveness to
a very intentional movement of the Holy Spirit who, like an eagle
with her young, disrupts the comfortable nest of our 'business
as usual' life and nudges us out into the adventure of an ever-
deepening relationship with Jesus and an ever more wholehearted
life. I wonder whether these restless yearnings may be our soul's
faint echoing of God's own yearnings for us and for the life he longs
for us to experience and live. It was Augustine who captured the
age-old truth: 'You have made us for yourself, and our hearts are
restless until they find their rest in you.' I believe that there are times
when, out of the strength of his passionate love for us, God gifts us
with a restlessness that can only be satisfied by himself, by a more
profound experience of his love, by a more vital experience of his
presence – giving purpose to our days, direction to our lives, rest for
our souls and freedom for all we have been created to be and to do.

The Bible is replete with grace-edged invitations, which draw us more fully into the life of God and into experiences of his love and purposes for us. Jesus put flesh on the bones of those invitations and gave them a voice. Over these past few years, as I've studied the invitations of Jesus sprinkled throughout the gospels, I've come to see that, in each of them, Jesus is offering us a richer, more authentic way to live; we are given the music and the words for a better song to sing.

It's the song that Jesus himself sang out with his life as he lived as a man – and as a child of the same God and Father who is ours too. It's the song of a grace-shaped, love-crafted, freedom-owned, God-dependent life. But Jesus is not only the way to this life; he *is* the life. He doesn't just sing the song; he himself *is* the song. Every invitation that Jesus holds out to us is an invitation to a deeper experience of his life permeating and saturating our own, transforming us into the men and the women we *know*, in the very depths of our being, we were created to be. Every invitation is an opportunity to allow him to be present in our lives in the fullness of who he is, to be drawn ever further into the adventure of knowing him, of loving him, of becoming more and more like him in every part of our being. Every invitation is an invitation to hope – that life really can be different; that a fuller, deeper, richer life can be more than a dream.

From the many invitations Jesus gave, we will focus on just six. In each of the chapters that follow we will unpack a single invitation, trusting that the Holy Spirit will draw us more deeply into understanding the life that Jesus wants to share with us, the life that God has on his heart for us to live.

Anthony de Mello once wryly commented that 'no one gets drunk on the word "wine"',[3] and we don't learn to sing our better song by just reading the words or by listening to the music – we learn to sing by singing. With this in mind, each chapter ends with a focused reflection, a prayer form or spiritual practice which may help us to engage more intentionally and personally with the particular invitation of that chapter. As we walk with Jesus through these words, I trust that we will discover new depths of energy and desire to live more fully, more freely, more courageously, more wholeheartedly Christlike lives. This is my hope-laden prayer for you as you read this book; it is the ongoing prayer for my life.

Before reading any further, it might be helpful to pause for a moment in God's presence; to bring yourself to him for all that he might want to do for you and in you as you read through this book. You might find it helpful to use the prayer below or allow it to be a springboard into your own prayer.

O Lord,
Hear the sighing longings of my soul
For more…
More life,
More love,
More freedom
To be
All that you desire for me.

O Lord,
Teach me a better song to sing.
Give me
An open ear to hear it and
Courage to sing it –
Not in some distant day
Or distant place,
But here, now,
On this day,
In this place.

O Lord,
Give me
Your song.
Amen

1

This is the life

'I have come that they may have life, and have it to the full.'
JOHN 10:10 (NIV)

The abundant life is an ordinary life transformed by the power of God through Jesus Christ living in us.
Stephen W. Smith[4]

Hanging in my bathroom is a canvas print depicting a scene of utter tranquillity. Dusk. Hints of pink and grey feathering the wisps of clouds reflected in the ripples of the lake. The dark silhouette of trees frame the outer borders and, peeking out at the bottom, the edges of a wind-weathered dock. Across those edges, the words, 'This is the life.' No exclamation mark needed; it's a statement of fact. The print was a gift from my friends Dave and Karen and is a precious reminder of my favourite place on earth – their summer cabin on the shores of Deer Lake in Minnesota. There have been so many times over the years when dusk has found me sitting in a canoe on that lake, my paddle resting across my knees, my whole being as hushed and as still as the lake itself, and I've whispered to myself, 'This is the life.'

But it's not.

It's a pause, a break, a moment of peace amid the busyness, the duties and the demands of the rest of life.

It may not be a canoe on a lake which draws these words out of us. It could be the exhilaration at the end of a run when the blood is pumping and we feel as though we are living on every cylinder God has given us. Closer to home, it could be the satisfaction of a cup of tea in the garden after a hard afternoon of digging and planting, or the joy of getting a group of family and friends together for a special occasion – and everyone is happy, no one is grumpy, the food is good, the wine is flowing and, as we look around, we sense those words rising from the depths of our hearts: 'This is the life.'

Each one of us probably has a picture that epitomises what that phrase means to us. It may not be hanging in our bathroom, but it's there, tucked away somewhere in a neglected corner of our minds and our hearts. It may represent our idea of the best life we can imagine living – until something happens (or doesn't happen) to wake us up to the possibility that perhaps there could be an even better life to live than the one we're currently living, one which has very little to do with what is going on 'out there' and much more to do with what is going on 'in here', in the depths of who I am.

Some while after my dad died, I asked my mother how she was feeling about her life. Her poignant response has stayed with me: 'My life is full, but my heart is empty.' We don't have to have lost a loved one to identify with those words. Our lives can be full of good and helpful things, our time may be spent well and productively, and yet we can feel like our hearts, our souls, the very core of who we are, are sometimes achingly empty.

There are times when, in the goodness of God, a shaft of truth comes breaking into our lives, showing us not just what our life is, but what it could be, what it might yet be. A while ago, I came across a poem by the American educator and author Dawna Markova, which, in the hands of the Holy Spirit, did exactly that for me. Her poem became a mirror of truth in which I caught a glimpse of the reality of my life at that time. Her words challenged me, unsettled me and stirred in me a longing to live differently – not to settle into complacency or compromise, but to move more surely into whatever life God had for me to live. Here are her words:

> I will not die an unlived life.
> I will not live in fear
> of falling or catching fire.
> I choose to inhabit my days,
> to allow my living to open me,
> to make me less afraid,
> more accessible,
> to loosen my heart
> until it becomes a wing,
> a torch, a promise.
> I choose to risk my significance;
> to live so that which came to me as seed
> goes to the next as blossom
> and that which came to me as blossom,
> goes on as fruit.[5]

Would I die an 'unlived life'? I hoped I wouldn't, but in the bright light of Markova's words I realised that, for the most part, I was living my life quite tentatively and guardedly. I saw that I was living an increasingly rushed life of duty and commitment, which seemed to be becoming narrower and less expansive with each passing year. I sensed a gradual wearing away of joy and hope – not huge, but experienced as a growing weariness and a staleness which seemed to linger around the edges of my days.

Markova's words stirred in me a longing to live with greater passion and purpose. Her words painted a picture of a life which wasn't governed by fear, but was open and vulnerable to others; which wasn't self-protective or hesitant, but willing to take risks, to grow and to change. This was not a tight, narrow life, but an expansively exuberant life, a wholehearted life that contributed something worthwhile and lasting to the lives of others. In this poem I saw flashes of truth, moments when light splashed across the words, and I caught glimpses of God's own desire for my own life. In no time at all, the Holy Spirit had scooped up the yearnings that had been brought to the surface by Markova's words and carried them – and me – into the presence of Jesus and the declared purpose of his coming: 'I have come that they may have life, and have it to the full' (John 10:10, NIV).

The heartbeat which pulses through all of Jesus' invitations is cradled within the declaration of these words – that we would experience the fullest and deepest and richest life imaginable. We may have read or heard these words so many times that we pass over them with hardly a second thought, but if we allow ourselves to hear them with the raw energy, freshness and passion with which Jesus spoke them, these words are dynamite. Exploding our complacency and complicity in living small, guarded lives, they drop us right into the throbbing heart of God's desire for us – life in all its fullness.

Different translations help in capturing the meaning of the words Jesus uses here:

> I came that they may have *and* enjoy life, and have it in abundance [to the full, till it overflows]. (AMP)

> My purpose is to give them a rich and satisfying life. (NLT)

> But I have come to *give you everything in abundance, more than you expect* – life in its fullness until you overflow! (TPT)

These words describe in no uncertain terms the kind of life that God wants for us, and it is far from a wearisome, carefully orchestrated life of sin-avoidance or sin-management. It goes beyond the pursuit of holiness and righteousness (as good as those pursuits are), and it goes beyond duty and discipline (as worthy as they are). Jesus' words hold out the hope of a richly textured wholeness for our lives, whatever the circumstances and wherever those lives are lived.

The *zoe* life

Read the Sunday supplements or flick through the magazines while waiting at your local surgery or hairdresser, and you'd be forgiven for believing that a rich, fulfilling and satisfying life consists of ticking goals off a bucket list, having enough money to guarantee a happy retirement or covering our walls with photos and certificates that show something about the way we've lived our lives, something of the achievements we've earned. We may be drawn to the well-touted benefits of mindfulness, yoga or a vegan diet, hoping that peace of mind and new energy will follow as we commit ourselves to these practices; and they often do, at least for a while.

We spend our money and our time learning how to live differently, how to live more satisfyingly and productively from whatever expert we trust. And all the while, in the pages of our Bibles, there is Jesus, holding out to us the offer of life in all its fullness and modelling for us what that life actually looks like – not within the walls of our churches on a Sunday morning, but in the places where most of us spend our days: among our families, in our place of work, in our relationships; amid conflict and challenges, needs and difficulties; amid the dailiness of a life lived in ordinary places.

In the New Testament three different Greek words are translated as 'life'. In John 10:10, the Greek word used is *zoe*. Piecing together a definition of this word from different Bible dictionaries, we learn that *zoe* is life that is nurtured and sustained by God's own life. It's life that comes from God himself. This God-sourced, God-sustained, God-infused life is what Jesus tells us he has come to give to us. But Jesus doesn't stop there; he hasn't come so that we could just have such a life, as stunning as that is in itself – but that we would have it 'abundantly'.

The word translated here as 'abundantly' means over and above, more than is necessary, overflowing. There is an exuberant extravagance bursting out of Jesus' words here. The picture Jesus paints for us is of a vibrantly authentic life, drenched by and overflowing with the life of God. When Jesus tells us that he has come so that we may have life in all its fullness, *this* is the life he is holding out to us: not an improved, reformed, upgraded version of our present lives, but a dynamically transformed life, wide open to God and to the glorious adventure of living life with him. In stark contrast to the Pharisees and the teachers of the law, whom Jesus describes as thieves and destroyers of life (John 10:10), Jesus emphatically declares that *he* has come so that we would experience 'more and better life than [we] ever dreamed of' (MSG). But we don't need to wonder or imagine what such a fully alive life might look like – we only have to look at Jesus, because *this* is the life that he himself lived as a human being; this is the life he invites *us* to live.

'Behold the man!'

Over 2,000 years ago, Pontius Pilate shouted to the gathered crowd, braying for Jesus' death, 'Behold the man!' (John 19:5, KJV). I doubt he had any idea what he was doing in drawing our attention to Jesus, because as we behold this man, we see the embodied reality of a life lived as God always intended a human life to be lived. In Jesus, we see a life filled with love and trusting dependence on God, with joy and peace and grace and truth, filled with mercy and tenderness, with passion and purpose.

The apostle John had many years to reflect on the life of Jesus, and after all of this reflection, he stated very simply, 'In him was life' (John 1:4, NIV). In him was *zoe*. In this one word, John is telling us that Jesus was bursting with the creative, nurturing, dynamic, compassionate, loving life of God; he was overflowing with that life. When people brushed up against Jesus, they came away dusted with the life of God; they experienced something of the rich fullness of the life of God breaking into their own lives at that point of contact. To their delighted surprise, they discovered that they were noticed and known, that they were seen and loved, that the concerns of their hearts mattered and that their small lives were part of a much grander purpose. They discovered that the God who created the heavens and the earth had appeared and opened wide his arms and his heart in the warmest of welcomes; and he did all this through the person of Jesus.

Even a cursory glance through the gospels, however, will reveal that Jesus didn't live this God-resplendent life in ideal circumstances, but in circumstances and in relationships which are not a million miles removed from the ones in which we may be living. One of my favourite verses in the whole of scripture is Hebrews 4:15, which, in the vivid words of *The Message*, tells us that Jesus is not 'out of touch with our reality' – but has lived that reality to the full. In Jesus, we have someone who perfectly understands the context of our lives because he has lived our lives; he has stood where we might one day stand; he has already faced what we might one day face. Reading through the gospel accounts of Jesus' life over the past months, I've been struck by the very real constraints and challenges he lived with – socially, physically, financially, relationally. He lived with the childhood experience of having been a refugee in an alien land; he lived with questions about his identity and slurs on his background which must have chafed and hurt. He was misrepresented and misunderstood. He was rejected, betrayed and abandoned. He knew heights of joy and depths of grief and agony.

In that same verse from Hebrews, the writer goes on to state that Jesus was tempted in exactly the same ways that we are tempted, which means that there is not a temptation that we have faced that he hasn't already faced. He knows all about the temptation to give in, to give up, to let go, to walk away. Jesus knew the temptation to doubt the goodness of God, to compromise God's word, to wonder if it will be worth it in the end. There is nothing in our lives, nothing in our circumstances, that Jesus does not know, does not understand, has not already faced and lived through. We are safe to come to him with all that we are, in all our brokenness and weakness, in our failures and our sin and our neediness, because we come to the one who reveals to us the heart of the God who has compassion on all that he has made, who remembers our frame, who knows we are just dust (Psalm 103:14). He never forgets who we are; he never forgets where we've come from; he never forgets what we face in our days. Ever.

As we study the life of Jesus and the contexts and circumstances in which he lived that life, it becomes clear that whatever abundant life is, it is not a life freed from suffering, pain and tragedy. It's not a life in which every desire is granted, every dream fulfilled. The reality is that loved ones still die, jobs are still lost, finances are still tight and the challenges of life are as real for the child of God as they are for anyone else. Things weren't easy for Jesus, and there are no guarantees that they will be easy for us. The abundant life which Jesus is holding out to us is not a Pollyanna life of perpetual sunshine, where no shadows are allowed to darken our days. It's not a life to be lived somehow *above* our circumstances, but *in* them. When we understand that this is the true nature of this abundant life, we no longer have to keep our struggles, our doubts and our fears hidden. We can begin to be honest with ourselves, with God and with others about where we really are in our life. This honesty clears a space for Jesus to come and stand with us in those harder places as a constant presence in the sometimes unfixable reality of our days, empowering us to live and to grow right there, in that very place, with courage and dignity and strength, and to discover that this kind of living, this kind of integrity, actually brings glory to God.

Fully alive!

Writing in the second century, one of the earliest church fathers, Irenaeus, wrote that 'the glory of God is a human being, fully alive'.[6] 'Glory' is not a word we use that often today. It means honour, splendour, beauty and worthiness all mixed up together into one concept. Irenaeus seems to be saying that the beauty, splendour and wonder of God can be seen in the life of a man or a woman who is fully alive. Centuries after Irenaeus wrote his words, the Westminster Shorter Catechism was composed. Its first question is: 'What is the chief end of man?' And the response is: 'Man's chief end is to glorify God, and to enjoy him forever'.[7]

Written in the 17th century, there is a confident clarity in these words. I wonder how we would answer if we were presented with that same question today? Depending on our experience of being discipled or our church tradition, we might answer that our chief end is 'to evangelise the lost', 'to make disciples of all nations' or 'to live a life of praise'. We might express our purpose and our calling as primarily serving God and his kingdom in some way. I remember as a young Christian being told by a more experienced Christian that I had been 'saved to serve'. You may have heard those words too. That little phrase shaped the early days of my faith journey and how I understood my relationship with God; I was his servant and my purpose in life was to serve. Jesus himself stated, 'I brought glory to you here on earth by completing the work you gave me to do' (John 17:4), and we do bring glory to God when we accomplish those 'good things' which God created *us* to do (Ephesians 2:10). But there's so much more than that!

When the composers of the Westminster Shorter Catechism wrote that we were 'to enjoy God forever', they took our lives out of the realm of duty and placed them firmly in the realm of delight. Synonyms of the word 'enjoy' include appreciate, love, relish and take delight or pleasure in. There is a warm energy to these words; they are engaging, relational, joy-bursting words! If we put this ancient confession of the church together with Irenaeus' words, we could say that our highest purpose in life, our greatest calling, is to bring glory to God by living fully alive, revelling in a joy-infused, loving relationship with God our Father, in which the purposes of his heart are fulfilled in us and through us.

It sounds great, doesn't it? But as I read through the gospels, it becomes so clear that there is no realistic way to live this kind of life except by allowing the indwelling Jesus to be himself in us; by allowing him to express the rich fullness of his life in and through our own unique personalities. In his classic book *Mere Christianity*, C.S. Lewis wrote, 'Every Christian is to become a little Christ. The whole purpose of becoming a Christian is simply nothing else.'[8] Strong and stark words – but as we study our Bibles, it becomes clear that our lives as Christians are not meant to be a 'Simon says' imitation of the life of Jesus; they are about the *embodiment* of the life of Jesus within our own lives. Perhaps they are not so much a 'what would Jesus do?' kind of life, as a 'what is Jesus, who is living in me, wanting to do in me and through me right now, right here?' kind of life.

Given everything we know about ourselves, however, the thought of our lives being an incarnation of the life of Jesus might seem an impossible goal – and it would be, were it not for two important truths.

The first is that we *are* actually indwelt by the resurrected Christ himself. It is such a mind-blowing truth that it can be really challenging for us to believe that Jesus, by his Spirit, lives within the very heart of our being. But it *is* true. Over and over again in his letters, the apostle Paul reminds us that believers in Jesus are truly indwelt by the very life of Jesus. For example, in 2 Corinthians 13:5 (NIV) Paul says, 'Do you not realise that *Christ Jesus is in you*?' In Galatians 2:20 he testifies to a truth about himself which is also true for us: 'It is no longer I who live, but *Christ lives in me*.' Paul's words in Colossians 2:19, captured so graphically in *The Message*, tell us about the 'Christ… whose very breath and blood *flow through us*'. And then, just a little earlier, in Colossians 1:27 (NIV), Paul reminds us, '*Christ in you*, the hope of glory' – the hope of becoming and being all that we long to be in the depths of our hearts but fear we may never be because we know who we are and who we've been. Our hope is not futile, because Jesus lives in us: not 'will live' sometime in the future when this earthly life has drawn its last breath, but now, as we sit reading these words, in whatever place we are in, in this very place, at this very time – Jesus is living in you, in me, which means that all that Jesus is – his faithfulness, his joy, his freedom, his courage and his confidence – is ours now and for always, because he lives in us.

Decades ago, Ruth Paxson captured the richness of this truth so vividly when she wrote: 'To be a Christian is nothing less than to have the glorified Christ living in us in actual presence, possession and power. It is to have him as the Life of our life... to have the divine seed which was planted in our innermost spirit blossoming out into growing conformity to his perfect life.'[9] More recently, Stephen W. Smith wrote in a simple, but reassuringly hopeful, statement for those of us who feel that our lives are not anything out of the ordinary: 'The abundant life is an ordinary life transformed by the power of God through Jesus Christ living in us.'[10]

The second truth which can infuse us with hope is that it is the declared intention of God's heart for us to become like his Son in every aspect of our being. Paul wrote, 'We see the original and intended shape of our lives there in him' (Romans 8:29, MSG). We don't need to guess at what God desires for our lives. We don't need to agonise over what God's purpose is for our lives. We don't need to imagine what our best life might be – we have only to lift up our heads and look at Jesus. Everything we could ever hope to be, everything we could ever imagine being, is seen there in him. Our hope of singing a better song is anchored in the confidence which Paul expressed when he wrote, 'And I am certain that God, who began the good work within you, will continue his work until it is finally finished on the day when Christ Jesus returns' (Philippians 1:6). God is totally and irrevocably committed to bringing to completion the work which he began in us the moment we became his own. It will take a lifetime, but he will do it. He is shaping our lives into the rich fullness of the life of Jesus. And it will be stunning.

Through the keyhole

I'm on the road a lot these days, travelling down the M4 from Gloucester to Wales to care for my elderly mother, who is very frail right now. I usually drive home on a Friday, and after a demanding week I'm usually tired. I know from experience that when I'm tired,

I'm not as patient with Mum as I should be. I'm not able to listen to her properly, and I'm not able to be as present to her and to her needs as I want to be. My mother lives just outside Swansea, and just as the steelworks of nearby Port Talbot come into view, I begin to pray a line from an old hymn by Frances Ridley Havergal: 'Live out thy life within me, O Jesus, King of kings.' I believe and trust that Jesus lives in me, so I pray this line, not just once on the drive to Wales, but many, many times over the course of the weekend.

I pray that the life of Jesus *within* me would be lived out *through* me. I know that on a Friday night, as I face the weekend, I do not have the energy or the resources to meet Mum's needs, but I know that Jesus does; I know that he is full of compassion and grace and patience and love and capacity for all that will be demanded of me. So I come to him with the scraping dryness of my need and this one-line prayer, and I ask him to be himself in me, to let *his* life flow unhindered through me, to make me conscious and responsive to the touch of his Spirit on my heart and will. And then I trust that he will do all that he can do and that he will give me the grace to do what I need to do.

But the sad truth is that I block the flow of Jesus' life in me so many times through my selfishness, unkindness, impatience and self-protectiveness – through all those moments when I choose to ignore the gentle promptings of his Spirit and choose my own way. But the moment I turn to Jesus in repentance, the moment I confess my sin and acknowledge my desperate need of him, the blockage seems to disappear. The power of his life flows again, and in a small Welsh village, the quiet joy of a weekend is restored, love is renewed and the life of Jesus is glimpsed, if only for a moment, in a shared meal in front of the television. It may not be glamorous, but it is real. This is the life; it really is.

Reflection: Fully alive

When Moses gathered the children of Israel together as they were about to enter the land that God had promised them, he spoke of a choice that they could make: 'Today I have given you the choice between life and death... Oh, that you would choose life' (Deuteronomy 30:19). Choosing life would mean that they were choosing to live within the love and care of God, who had led them out of the place of their slavery and was leading them into the fulfilment of their promised freedom. It would mean believing and behaving in line with the good intent of God's heart towards them. It would seem like a no-brainer of a choice – and yet as we follow the journey of these children of God after their entry into the promised land, we see that, in actual fact, they chose death. They didn't wander into it; the slow death of their souls as individuals and as a nation began when they deliberately chose to follow other gods, when they pursued other means of satisfying their needs, their desire for life. Over time they became idol worshippers, believing the lie that life would be found by carving it out for themselves, in independence from the God who had promised them so much – if they only trusted him to deliver it in his way and in his time. But they were impatient and figured they could make life work on their own terms. And we can be no different.

We are children of God; we have been drawn into the very life of God through Jesus; we have been offered the richest possible life as we trust Jesus to live out his life within us to the fullest measure of who he is. And yet so often, somewhere in the depth of who we are, we choose differently. We may have different reasons for our choice, but sometimes our doubt that Jesus really does live in us and that he can release his life in us causes us to look elsewhere for life; we make our own idols, not out of wood or stone, but out of the raw material of our relationships, our careers, our possessions, our achievements. We can even make the nurturing of our spiritual lives into an idol, constantly pursuing different spiritual experiences, looking for the next spiritual high, all in the hope of satisfying our thirst for life as we hoped it would be for us. We know that these 'idols' cannot ultimately bring us the life we long for, but we try. In our fear that what Jesus promises us may not be enough to satisfy our hearts, we give ourselves to those substitutes in the hope that, in exchange, they will give us what we need. But they can't. And they don't. And our lives will be no different from what they are now if we believe that they can.

Some of us may not be clinging to idols, but we may be cradling a false hope, shaped by the words, 'My life will begin when…' I wonder what our life is on hold for. Marriage? Children? A better job? A more effective treatment? Many of us park our lives in the car park of 'when' and we wait; and all the while life beckons and waves to us – and we look away.

Over many years of walking with Jesus, I've learnt that we don't just drift into the life that Jesus wants us to experience; we need to be intentional about our desire for such a life. We need to deliberately '*choose* life'; no one can choose life for us. We also need to be intentional about understanding whatever it is that may keep us from experiencing such a life. Reflecting on the following questions may help us to discern where we are right now, where we hope to be in our journey into this richest of lives and perhaps how we might move towards it more surely.

- What words would you use to describe your life right now?
  - As you look at those words, are there any that you would like to change, e.g. from 'overwhelmed' to 'free', from 'fearful' to 'peace-filled'.

- What would a 'fully alive' you look like in the context of the circumstances and the commitments that are your life right now?
  - Be bold! Paint a word picture – or an actual picture – of your life as a fully alive person. You may not be able to change your circumstances or your commitments – especially family ones – but you may be able to live differently within those places as you live more fully alive.

- ○ It may help to begin your reflection with the words, 'If I were fully alive, I would be…'

- Who are the people, where are the places, what are the activities or the spiritual practices which bring you into experiencing something of this life, which bring energy and vitality and the hope of transformation to you? How could you be more intentional about spending time with those people, in those places, doing those activities and engaging in those spiritual practices? What could that look like over the course of the next few months?

'*Christ lives in you*' (Colossians 1:27). This explosive truth is our hope of living fully alive, of becoming the person we most want to be and who God purposes for us to be. As an act of trust, you may want to make this truth into a prayer of thanksgiving and hope. Perhaps the prayer below might be a springboard for your own prayer.

Lord Jesus, you live within the very heart of me; you are alive in me. Live out your life in me. Live out in me your love and your compassion, your kindness and your truth, your trust in God and your joy in life. Bring me to life; bring me to the fullness of life which brings glory to you. Amen

2

Inward-bound

Then Jesus shouted, 'Lazarus, come out!' And the dead man came out, his hands and feet bound in graveclothes, his face wrapped in a headcloth. Jesus told them, 'Unwrap him and let him go!'

JOHN 11:43–44

I am finding it helpful to look at the grave clothes as things that are actually preventing me from what I desire most: freedom, life, and transformation.[11]

If the BBC were to make a film of this incident in John's gospel, I wonder if they might plot it as a dramatic story of disappointment and bewilderment, of agonised waiting and tragic death, leading up to the climactic moment when Jesus shouts out the name of his friend, 'Lazarus', and then to the accompaniment of a drum-rolling crescendo, the words 'Come out!' – and the dead man shuffles out – alive! Lazarus is rescued from the grave and raised to new life by the power of Jesus' word. In an unbelievable turn of events, weeping is turned to wonderment, disappointment to delight, anguish to awe.

Just moments before, Lazarus' sister Martha had confronted Jesus with a grief-soaked statement of fact, 'If only you had been here, my brother would not have died' (John 11:32). In response, Jesus declared a truth which he would shortly prove before her very eyes: 'I am the resurrection and the life' (John 11:25). Then, with tears in his eyes, he stood before the tomb of his friend and called out his name, summoning life out of death, the power of his word reaching into the tomb, grabbing Lazarus and pulling him back into life. It is a triumphant moment which those sisters, even in their wildest dreams, could never have imagined when their brother was laid in that tomb four days previously: the 'if only' of desperate disappointment swallowed up by the presence of a love stronger than death.

Jesus' shout to Lazarus here is so reminiscent of the words of Isaiah 49:9, where God shouts to the prisoners of darkness, 'Come out! I am giving you your freedom!' (TLB). All who are held captive are freed by that word. In some ways, this raising of Lazarus foreshadows the sure fulfilment of promises made earlier by Jesus that 'a time is coming when all who are in their graves will hear his voice and come out' (John 5:28–29, NIV); he tells us that the shepherd 'calls his own sheep by name and leads them out' (John 10:3). And here we have Lazarus, called by name, being led out of the tomb by the power of Jesus' word, stumbling out of the darkness, out of that death-cradling place. He was truly alive, but he was going nowhere while still swaddled in those grave clothes.

Lazarus probably heard Jesus' words as a command which cut through the cords of death that were holding him; his response to that command brought him back to life. My guess is that if we have heard a similar call to life, we probably didn't hear it as a command which demanded obedience, but as a compelling invitation to enter into a relationship with Jesus which opened up to us the expanse of his life-giving grace and ushered us into the adventure of a new way of living.

Although we were not wrapped in physical grave clothes on the day we responded to Jesus' call, the reality is that each one of us came into our new life a bit like Lazarus leaving the tomb that day, with life-limiting attitudes, beliefs and behaviours which were every bit as real as the grave clothes in which Lazarus was wrapped. The uncomfortable truth is that, even after years of knowing Jesus, there can be areas of our lives where we are as bound as Lazarus was at that moment. He was bound for just four days, but we may have been bound for years by our own grave clothes. And during those years, some of those clothes have become like second skins to us; we have become so accustomed to their presence that we are hardly aware of the way they are restricting us from living the life that Jesus promised us.

In a letter to the early disciples, the apostle John wrote that 'those who say they live in God should live their lives as Jesus did' (1 John 2:6), or as one contemporary translation puts it, 'The one who says he belongs to Christ should live the same kind of life Christ lived' (NLV). John seems to be stating that it's not just a question of being *alive* with the life of Jesus, but of *living* the life of Jesus, living *out* the life of Jesus in the dailiness of our relationships, our jobs, our everyday ordinary lives. Who doesn't want this? Who doesn't want our days to be lived as Jesus lived his days – with grace and love and passion and purpose and an intimacy with God that satisfies the very depths of who we are and fuels the richest of lives? We are back to incarnation – and the challenge to live out the life of Christ within. This may be the longing of our hearts – we want to live like Jesus – yet as deep as that longing is, perhaps even deeper is the frustration and disappointment that this is not our lives; this is not the reality of our days. We know something is out of kilter – we just aren't sure what it is or how to straighten it out.

Having tried to do more of everything we have been taught to do – reading our Bibles more, praying more, serving more – and discovering that those tried-and-trusted practices don't seem to work for us in the same way that they once did, we may come to the conclusion that there must be something 'out there' which is to blame for the muted life that we are experiencing. We may blame the pressures of our jobs, the challenges of our family situation or our church and its lack of sparkle and spirit. All of these may be contributing factors to our sense of restless dissatisfaction, but I wonder if the presence of certain grave clothes in our lives may be the cause of much of our disappointment with life, with God, with ourselves.

In writing of his own experience, Stephen W. Smith states, 'I am finding it helpful to look at the grave clothes as things that are actually preventing me from what I desire most: freedom, life, and transformation. Each grave-cloth can become a symbol of something that is inhibiting our movement forward, restricting us from experiencing the life that Jesus promises and robbing us of the possibilities of transformation.'[12]

Binding grave clothes

The scriptures are not silent about the grave clothes of our lives. They testify to the grave clothes of worry and anxiety, and our distracted absorption with 'the cares of this life' in all the forms in which they appear (Luke 8:14). There is sin which entangles or trips us up (Hebrews 12:1) and ungodly vows and rash promises which trap us into ways of behaving which can have disastrous consequences (1 Samuel 14:24). There are the tight bindings of legalism and a performance-based relationship with God (Galatians 5:1–4). There are regrets from the past and fears for the future which keep us from living fully in the present. We may be bound by longings for what might never be, prevented from living life now by what never was. More broadly, there are the tattered threads of the hyphenated self: self-righteousness, self-importance, self-defensiveness, self-absorption, self-satisfaction and all the other self-focused ways in which we try to make life work for us.

Recently I was reflecting on David's testimony that 'the ropes of death entangled me' (Psalm 18:4), and I wondered what the 'ropes of death' were in my life. What was I being tangled up in which robbed me of life? Something I've come to realise is that the ropes which bind us don't have to be the equivalent of thick cords. Physically, a single cotton or silk thread, wrapped many times around a body, can be as binding and imprisoning as any rope (think of Gulliver and the Lilliputians!). Spiritually, one small lie that we believe about ourselves or another person or God himself, repeated often enough, can become a cord of death to us. One destructive habit repeated often enough can suffocate healthy life in us. One hurtful comment rehearsed over and over again can cause us to be bound by bitterness, or self-pity, anger, resentment, sadness or anxiety for years. Our grave clothes may be woven from multi-stranded memories of past hurts, rejection, abuse, loss, guilt or heart-breaking regret. All that is unresolved, unforgiven or unhealed in our past can rob us of our freedom, our hope for the future, our experience of good in the present. These tensile threads can encircle our souls until we can hardly breathe with the tightness of their grip – and before we know it, we are inwardly bound and captive, living tight, constrained lives.

But intriguingly, we can be bound by good things too. We may be bound by ways of living or working or being that have stood us well in the past, but which we may need to let go of if we are to be truly free for what may lie ahead. There may be ways of relating to the Lord, or of worshipping, or areas of service, for example, that we have enjoyed for years, and yet we may sense that the Lord is tugging at the sleeve of those familiar clothes, and it's not comfortable. It is like a pair of old shoes that suddenly feel tight and pinching, but rather than buy new shoes, we hobble around in what no longer fits, because – well – we've always worn these shoes; they are familiar, we've been through a lot together and we've made lasting memories. We may not be able to run or dance so easily anymore, and our hips may ache because we're out of alignment – but we are not abandoning these shoes; we've worn them too long. Like Martha in her kitchen, we may be so entrenched in our understanding of how to serve the Lord, so entrenched in how we do life, that we may miss something new and fresh that God wants to give us. We might actually miss the 'better thing' (Luke 10:42) he has for us because we won't take off our old shoes!

The most stubborn strips

We don't know how long it took to unwrap Lazarus from his grave clothes, and in our own lives we can't set limits for how long it should take before we are free of our own grave clothes. In my own experience, there are times when the grave clothes fall off with barely a move on our part; times when the Spirit of God moves in power into our lives in a special way, and bindings which have hindered us for years are dealt with in an instant. In one grace-anointed moment we are released – and it is wonderful. But it is also true that most of us had been dead in sin for a long time before we received new life from Jesus, and removing the decaying grave clothes from those days is a slower process. If, for example, we spent years dead in sexual sin, perfectionism, anger, greed or jealousy, most of us probably won't experience immediate release from the well-established patterns of behaviour which are wrapped up with those grave clothes. Paul writes that we are 'being renewed' (2 Corinthians 4:16), we are 'being transformed' (Romans 12:2) and we 'are being transformed into the same image from one degree of glory to another' (2 Corinthians 3:18, ESV). These are progressive verbs, and they speak of the passing of time and of process – a Spirit-directed and often slow process of beginning to understand ourselves more deeply, of trusting God for his timing and his ways of releasing us, of cooperating with the Holy Spirit as he reveals to us our part in this process.

Of the many grave clothes we may have gathered around us in our journey through life, some seem to cling far more stubbornly, are closer to the skin of who we are and are so much harder to remove than the seemingly looser ones from the early days of our faith journey. It is these grave clothes that probably need our closest attention if we are to fully live the life that, in the depths of our hearts, we know is there, waiting for us to claim as our own. These particular grave clothes demand a depth of patience, wisdom and courage if we are to see them removed. In my experience of walking with others in their faith journeys, three of the most life-limiting cloths which have bound so many of us – and which may still bind us today – are disappointment, self-rejection and shame

Disappointment

The Oxford English Dictionary rather clinically defines disappointment as 'sadness or displeasure caused by the non-fulfilment of one's hopes or expectations'. Every single one of us lives with disappointment in one or more areas of our lives. It is part of being human to have expectations, and it is part of our human experience to have those expectations unfulfilled. As Paula Rinehart succinctly comments, 'In a fallen world, disappointment is a given.'[13] We don't have to have lived very long to know that this is true, so we may feel that the grave cloth of disappointment is such a normal part of life that we just need to learn to live with it. But when we do not process our disappointments appropriately, they may spiral down into darker emotions and behaviours which can seriously damage the health of our souls and threaten the flourishing of the life of Jesus in us and through us.

Doing an online search for the word 'disappointment' produced a list of synonyms which began gently enough with 'sadness, regret, dismay', but then became more emotionally laden: 'disillusionment, disenchantment, despondency, discontent, depression'. We are all familiar with small disappointments: the late arrival of a gift ordered for a child's birthday, a restaurant treat that was not all it was advertised to be, the interruption of a day we'd planned for work on the house. Faced with such disappointments, we usually just have a small moan, accept them and move on. Then there are the more significant disappointments: a job promotion which never materialised, a relationship which promised much but went nowhere, a medical condition which no amount of treatment seems to fix. The list goes on. These disappointments may cause us some distress and grief, but they are not usually a danger to the health of our souls unless we lay the blame for those disappointments at the feet of God.

In the early days of our faith, we are rarely disappointed with God. We pray – God answers. We pray again – and God answers again. Over time, we bank enough experience of God's faithfulness in answering our prayers that our expectations become the legal tender with which we trade. So we pray, and we expect God to answer, but as we grow in our faith we may be surprised at the increasing number of times that God doesn't answer our prayers, at least in the ways we expected. This can be deeply distressing, for us unless we recognise that one of the ways in which God expands our understanding of who he is and what sharing his life is all about is to take the spade of disappointment and dig us out of our entrenchments and our immature understandings of how life should work for us as believers in Jesus. The truth is that the disappointments of our lives are so often the means by which God prepares our hearts for a more transformative encounter with the fullest dimensions of who he is. When we can acknowledge our disappointments and surrender them into God's hands, we discover that God uses those very disappointments to shake the status quo of our lives, clearing space for something new, something we might never have expected.

Martha and Mary may have experienced the shock of being disappointed with Jesus, evidenced in their words 'if only you had been here' (John 11:21, 32). They had sent word to Jesus that 'your dear friend is very sick' (John 11:3). There was an expectation that he would come, that his love for his friend Lazarus would move him to drop whatever he was doing and come immediately to the rescue. They made no demand of him, no request; they just informed him of the situation. But implicit in that was an expectation, and it was disappointed to death.

'*If only…*' I wonder if we have sighed and sobbed those same words to Jesus, when, like Martha and Mary, we have brought our needs to him, when we have laid out our pain, our confusion, our agonised questions, when we have unwrapped before him whatever it is that is breaking our heart, racking our brains – only to find silence. Not the reassurance of his presence, not the answer to prayer that we had hoped for or expected, just – nothing. We have done our bit, we have prayed and trusted, but the job offer does not appear, the marriage does not survive, the cancer continues to devour and wars do not cease around the world. Bereft of hope, our disappointments shape the words, 'if only...' And it seems there is no way out: not now. It is too late.

And yet, if this account tells us anything, it tells us that the timing of Jesus' response to our prayers is neither arbitrary nor capricious. The circumstances of our lives and how they are played out are not incidental to the purposes of God for our lives, but they are woven into those purposes in ways that we might barely, if ever, discern – at least in this life. But for now, there is the invitation to trust the kind intent of the heart of God towards us that, even in these circumstances, life will lift its head again – perhaps not in the way we have imagined, but in ways that will eventually cause us to bow our heads in wonder at the goodness of God revealed in our lives.

As I've reflected on the difference between the disappointments which leave us distressed or confused for a while, and those which seem to leave us deeply wounded and hardly able to carry on, I've wondered at the role played by doubt, particularly doubt in the character of God. When our disappointments nudge us – or sometimes hurl us – into doubting the character of God, then we are on the slippery slope into the darker 'D's of discouragement, depression and despair. Our disappointments with the circumstances of our lives, with our marriages, children, jobs and colleagues, with prayers that have not been answered as we expected or hoped, with ideal homes which spring leaks and workmen who don't know how to fix them – these have the potential to provoke us into doubting that God cares for us, that God can protect us and provide for us, that he is truly concerned for our lives.

When the foundations of our faith are pounded by the sledgehammer of doubt, then discouragement can easily set in. If we were to deconstruct the word discouragement, we would discover that the middle part of the word is adopted from the French, *coeur*, which means 'heart', and that dis*cour*agement literally means to take the heart out of a person. Discouragement can suck the heart out of us, leaving us weak, lacking in courage and vulnerable to the next of the 'Deadly Ds': depression.

When our spirits are bowed down low within us, when our whole experience of life is muted, when life seems heavy and we are so weary of trying to lift it above the waterline of our faith that we might just let it all go – then we may be experiencing the mind-numbing reality of depression. If we do not have help at this point, this depression can become heavier and more dense until we find ourselves pushed down, plunged into the darkness of despair, the awfulness of believing that there is no hope for our lives, nowhere left to go, nothing left to do that can make any difference to where we are. We are stuck. We are at the bottom of a very deep well, at night, with no rope and no one around to throw us a rope, even if there was one.

This is where we find the apostle Paul in 2 Corinthians. The deep disappointment of his treatment in Asia had led him eventually to this place of awful despair. He writes, 'We were crushed and overwhelmed beyond our ability to endure, and we thought we would never live through it' (2 Corinthians 1:8). Or, as the AMPC puts it: 'We were so utterly and unbearably weighed down *and* crushed that we despaired even of life [itself].' He was in a truly desperate place. But there was a truth that Paul grabbed on to at this time which brought him gasping to the surface of his faith: Paul believed that God 'raises the dead' (2 Corinthians 1:9). Beyond grief and disappointment and despair – and even death – was this hope-forged truth. He may have been sinking into despair, but he reached up and grasped the rope of the truth of who God was and what God was able to do – and he hung on.

As we watch the ways in which Martha and Mary handle their disap-pointment at Jesus' non-arrival at their brother's bedside when they needed him, one thing is clear – they didn't hide that disappointment but brought it directly to Jesus himself. Their words 'if only you had been here' are as much a reflection of their faith as they are an implied rebuke at his failure to turn up according to their timetable.

'Trust in him at all times, O people. Pour out your heart before him. God is a safe place for us.' David's words in Psalm 62:8 (NLV) encourage us to pour out our hearts to God until there is nothing left to say. The scriptures are full of the cries of God's disappointed people. As they poured out their hearts to him in lament, they discovered God was a safe place for them. And they found that he embraced both them and their disappointments, holding them tight in the assurance of his knowledge, wisdom, purpose, goodness and love – giving them hope for the future and for what might yet be. Rather than taking them away from God, away from life, their disappointments became the pathways which led them into his presence and, eventually, into a richer experience of life and freedom. It can be so for us too, as we open up to him and trust him with the truth of our disappointments.

Self-rejection

The plea for prayer came in a text message from a friend concerned about a woman in her Bible study group. For months, Jo had been making giant steps towards God, towards greater mental and emotional and spiritual health. Sarah's message was brief: 'Jo is not doing so well right now; yesterday she told me she's quitting the group because no matter how hard she tries, she just doesn't have what it takes to be a real Christian. Please pray.'

The grave cloth of self-rejection can choke the life out of us. Jo is being suffocated by the weight of her self-rejection, by her shrouding sense of inadequacy. Self-rejection is not simply about not liking how we look, being negative about our abilities or wishing we had a different personality; it's actually far more serious than that, because it is ultimately rooted in a rejection of who God says we are. Henri

Nouwen went so far as to describe self-rejection as 'the greatest enemy of the spiritual life, because it contradicts the sacred voice that calls us "The Beloved"'.[14] Our self-rejection can be a stubborn refusal to accept God's evaluation of us as worthy of love and affection, a subtle but profound unwillingness to trust his heart or to believe his word that we are his masterpiece (see Ephesians 2:10), a unique manifestation of the mind and heart and purposes of God in this world.

Shortly before his death, theologian Donald Nicholl recounted the following story: 'It was one of those dreadful meetings where we all had to introduce ourselves. The others all introduced themselves by their jobs and professions. When it came to my turn, all I wanted to say was: "My name is Donald. I am a unique manifestation of God."'[15] It was a declaration of a truth that he had made his own – and boldly lived out!

Perhaps the tragedy of our unwillingness to trust God and his word is the contrasting willingness that many of us have to trust the diminishing and life-snatching words we may have heard about ourselves from those we have allowed into our lives as adults or who were present in our lives as children. We may have trusted the words of authority figures such as parents, teachers, colleagues and people in ministry who have said unkind or negative things – either to us directly or to others about us. We may have taken to heart the words of friends or relatives who have casually and often unknowingly damaged us with seemingly innocuous comments which have nestled into the crevices of our innermost hearts and which have contributed to our self-rejection: 'John's never been good at...'; 'Mary's hopeless at...'

Over time, we may have come to believe these evaluations and owned them for ourselves, trusting a second-hand 'truth' which God has never uttered about us, but which is now woven into the very fabric of the cloth we wrap around our self-rejecting self, a cloth which grows tighter and tighter as the years go by. It is a cloth which originates in a place of death, spun by the father of lies and the accuser of the brethren. It is a cloth that suffocates the life out of us. Over time, we may build up a dossier of compelling evidence which validates our conviction that we are not worth the love and acceptance of God. Our resolute self-rejection only anticipates the rejection we are sure we will one day receive from God when he wakes up to who we really are.

Regardless of the source of our self-rejection, we need to be aware that self-rejection can be deceptively and surprisingly prideful, because it elevates what we believe about ourselves above what God has declared to be true about us. Stripped of the many justifications that we can muster in defence of our position, at its heart, self-rejection is an assault on the character of God, on his loving creation of us, on his delight in us. If we persist in clinging to it, it will rob us of our dignity, it will profoundly diminish our sense of worth and it may eventually erode our trust in the goodness of God.

Self-rejection can blight our experience of the life that Jesus has given us, leaving us feeling despondent, defeated and doubtful that there could ever be another way to live. Self-rejection can become a distorted lens through which we view everything about our lives, our circumstances, our failures and our mistakes. Our self-rejection conspires against us – extinguishing any spark of hope we might have for change. But there *is* hope of change, and that comes as we determine to embrace the truth of who God says we are, as we commit ourselves to viewing our lives through the lens of such words as those found in Isaiah 43:4 (ESV), for example, where God states, 'You are precious in my eyes, and honoured, and I love you.' Somewhere in the depths of our hearts, we need to agree to be the person we already are in his eyes.

Over the years, I've had many conversations with men and women who are distressingly and determinedly self-rejecting. After some time – often weeks – of sharing and praying, and when I've sensed that they might be willing to do so, I have suggested that at the start of every day they speak out loud the following sentence: 'I am truly known, completely accepted and dearly loved by God, and I please him just by breathing!' For some, speaking these words was excruciatingly difficult – to the point of tears. But as they persisted for weeks and sometimes months, they experienced real change in their relationship with God, in their understanding of themselves and in their experience of living within the generous grace of Christ. Slowly, the truths which they spoke and heard entered into their hearts where they began to settle as convictions, displacing the lies and the fears that were occupying space there. I've seen this transformation happen many times now, and I've come to believe that the grave cloth of self-rejection can only ever be stripped away by our embrace of the truth of God's grace-filled love and acceptance of us.

But accepting God's acceptance of us can be a scary prospect, because it demands that we trust, that we let go of all we have truly deep down believed about ourselves and about God and take the risk that God is not going to back down or back away, or back out of his commitment to us – ever. One of the first verses I memorised as a new Christian was Hebrews 13:5, which in the AMP states, 'For he has said, "I will never [under any circumstances] desert you [nor give you up nor leave you without support, nor will I in any degree leave you helpless], nor will I forsake *or* let you down *or* relax my hold on you [assuredly not]!' Another verse which strengthened my confidence was God's assurance in Isaiah 54:10 (ESV) that 'the mountains may depart and the hills be removed, but my steadfast love shall not depart from you'. For some of us, believing these words at a heart level, not just in our heads, can be a big ask, but when we begin to trust the acceptance of God, little by little the cloth of self-rejection becomes looser and looser, and we become more and more free to live – really live.

We may reject our bad parts, but perversely, we can reject the good parts too. I heard of a nun who, in contrast to Donald Nicholl's hearty declaration of his uniqueness, struggled to believe she was in any way special. Her Mother Superior ordered her to pray the following prayer every day until told to stop: 'Help me, God, to accept the truth about myself – no matter how beautiful it is!' Some of us may need to pray such a prayer as an act of faith, acknowledging to God and to ourselves the truth that we are 'fearfully and wonderfully made' (Psalm 139:14, NIV).

So many of us cringe at saying anything good or complimentary about ourselves, our gifts and strengths, or areas of encouraging growth in our lives. Those of us who are British may use the excuse that to behave any differently is very un-British. I'm so glad Jesus wasn't British! As I read through John's gospel particularly, I encounter a Jesus who is so free, so completely unembarrassed by his gifts and his uniqueness. He says: 'I am the bread of life' (John 6:35), 'I am the way, the truth, and the life' (John 14:6) and 'I am the light of the world' (John 8:12). Jesus is fully accepting of the wonder that he is. His attitude reminds me that the psalmist not only declares that he is 'fearfully and wonderfully made' but also 'that [his] soul knoweth right well' (Psalm 139:14, KJV).

What does our soul know and acknowledge about us? Perhaps we need to be more like Jesus here and, if not in public, at least in our personal times in God's presence, thank him for the gifts and strengths that we have been given. Thank him for the wonder of our uniqueness and the ways in which he uses that uniqueness to bless other people's lives. This might slowly but surely turn the kaleidoscope of our image of ourselves more into alignment with the image held by the one who unashamedly declares for time and eternity, 'You are all beautiful, my love. You are perfect' (Song of Solomon 4:7, NLV).

Shame

Once, when I was about eight years old, my grandmother began to beat her head against the kitchen wall and, as she did so, pointedly told me it was my fault; I was to blame for her actions. I couldn't think of anything I had done that would make her act so desperately, so I don't remember feeling guilty, but I do remember a slow burning flush of shame creeping up my neck and into my face as I realised that there was something so badly wrong with me that my very existence had provoked my grandmother to hurt herself in this way. As an adult looking back on that incident, I wonder at the misery that was in my grandmother's life which pushed her towards such a desperate action and such cruel words. But I grieve too for the tender-hearted little girl that I was then and the blame-laden accusation which was such an awful burden to carry – and which I *did* carry for years.

Looking back, I can see how the weight of my grandmother's blame and the shame I experienced at that time began to shape my soul into the sometimes overly responsible, overly conscientious adult I became. I came to believe that when anything went wrong in the lives of those I cared about, somehow, it was my fault – even if I was half a world away, somehow I was to blame. And there was nothing I could do to make it right, to fix it, to make it better. I was just not good enough.

Many of us have had similar childhood experiences of shame, if not within the context of the family, then in the classroom or the playground, on the sports field or in a holiday club, in the many contexts where vulnerable children are brought face-to-face with the potential to be deeply shamed, to carry blame that is not theirs to carry. The findings of those who study shame and its impact upon the shaping of a personality suggest that much of our adult sense of shame is nurtured in early childhood experiences of being shamed for something that we did or did not do. The ways in which we have internalised that shame has had a significant role in shaping how we view ourselves and our place in the world.

But there are other sources for the shame we carry around with us. As we read our Bibles, we see clearly that there is a shame that arises from actions which have compromised God's word and our integrity in some ways. The very earliest example we have of this is in the account of Adam and Eve and their encounter with the serpent who persuaded Eve that God was lying to her (Genesis 3:4), that God was holding out on her by denying her access to something which could make her God-like in her understanding of the world. Eve and her husband ate the fruit they had been forbidden to eat and, because of that one awful, irretrievable act, innocence was forever lost: 'At that moment their eyes were opened, and they suddenly felt shame at their nakedness. So they sewed fig leaves together to cover themselves' (Genesis 3:7). They hid from themselves and they hid from God. Before that act, they 'were both naked, but they felt no shame' (Genesis 2:25), but the hijacking of their trust in God's character and his word led to a deep shame about who they were and a desire to cover that up. It also led to the first experience of blame, as Adam blamed Eve (and God too, for giving him Eve), and Eve blamed the serpent for all that had happened.

In our own experience as redeemed children of God, we may sin, feel guilty for what we've done and perhaps be ashamed of who we are. When that awareness leads us into the presence of God and into receiving his forgiveness, cleansing and restoration, then guilt and shame have done their job; they have exercised a legitimate role in our lives. But it is possible for shame to exercise an illegitimate and pernicious role in our lives which must break the heart of God as he sees the effect it has on us.

Shame's bullying role in shaping our lives seems to begin as a toxic lie that burrows its way into our soul and settles there with devastating effect. That lie is that we are not and never can be enough – for God, for ourselves or for the people we care about. We cannot be good enough, wise enough, godly enough, kind enough, thin enough, bright enough – the list goes on... and on. Through the circumstances of our lives and, more importantly, how we have interpreted those circumstances, we may have come to believe that we are irreparably defective and lacking whatever it is that is needed from us to be acceptable and approved and loved. Brené Brown, in her groundbreaking work on shame, defines it as 'the intensely painful feeling or experience of believing we are flawed and therefore unworthy of love, belonging and connection'.[16] Elsewhere she writes about the ways in which we try to handle this shame by seeking safety in pretence and perfection: 'If I look perfect, and do everything perfectly, I can avoid or minimize the painful feelings of shame, judgment, and blame.'[17]

I so understand the lure of perfectionism as a protection against the stinging smacks of shame on our souls, but the truth is that perfection is an unrealistic goal. When we believe that only perfection is acceptable, that our perfect performance is the only thing which will guarantee us the acceptance and approval and sense of worth and value which we were designed to receive from God, then our failure to be perfect will lead us further into the sucking quagmire of shame. And the cycle continues: we sin, we feel guilt and shame, we hide from God and others under quilted layers of perfectionism and performance – which we eventually fail at – so again, we feel guilt and shame. Thankfully, we have a God who is able to reach into whatever miry bog has sucked us in, pull us out and stand us on the solid, unshakeable ground of his age-long love, his endless faithfulness, his overwhelming grace towards us.

John Ortberg wrote that 'we live in the unceasing care of a relentlessly attentive and gracious God'.[18] This one wise line is a gift to all of us who are wrapped in the grave cloth of shame, because it reminds us that our lives are not to be lived in fear of being discovered in the place of our shame and of being dis-graced there; they are to be lived within the tender, attentive care of a grace-filled God. And that makes all the difference.

The answer to the debilitating and restrictive grip of shame on our lives is to be held in the grip of the truth of our complete acceptance in Christ (Ephesians 1:6), that we belong, forever, to him (Isaiah 43:1), that we are totally known (Psalm 139) and understood (Hebrews 4:15–16), that all our inadequacy is met by the greatness of his adequacy (2 Corinthians 3:5), and that we can be all that we ever hoped to be, because our failures can never distance us from the God who 'knows our frame' and 'remembers that we are dust' (Psalm 103:14, ESV). These truths are like sharpened tools that can, with time, cut away the most stubborn of grave clothes – not just those of shame, but all the other ones too. And God often hands those tools to other people in our lives to help set us free.

Unwrap him!

As the newly risen but still bound Lazarus stood in the warm sunshine that day, Jesus turned to those standing around and told them to unwrap him and let him go. These were not specialist grave-clothes unwrappers! In fact, none of them would ever have unwrapped a newly risen man before; but the grave clothes were there, right before them, and Jesus seemed confident that these ordinary men and women could do the job.

In those circumstances, Lazarus could not unwrap or free himself from his grave clothes; he needed help. And it's this help that may be just what we need. For most of us, we would rather be the one who unwraps than the one who is needing to be unwrapped. To be open and honest about our grave clothes, both with ourselves and with someone we trust, will demand a certain amount of courage. We will need to be willing to peel off our masks of competence and independence and be seen as the needy and imperfect men and women we really are – and that is not a comfortable place for most of us. We would much rather be seen as capable and strong and able to handle our lives without anyone else's help, but the truth is that we need each other; we need each other's' wisdom, love and hope. Sometimes that will mean we are the recipient of the gracious ministry of unwrapping, and at other times we may be the unwrappers.

A truism of any community of believers is that every single one of us is walking around, trailing some kind of grave cloth. Possibly one of the most profound privileges we have within our friendships, our fellowships and our church communities is that of offering grace and love and acceptance to one another, coming alongside each other and, under the guidance of the Holy Spirit, helping in the removal of our binding grave clothes. Practically, we do this unwrapping through prayer, through listening, through offering wise counsel and through skilful intervention. We do it through kind and discerning questions and through the willingness to stay with a person where they are in their wrapped-up lives, living alongside them as bringers of hope and light and truth, for however long the Lord may ask us to be there.[19]

We cannot sing a better song while we are still wrapped in our grave clothes, our voices stifled by their tight, restrictive grip on us. We may be aware that there are habits of thought and practice which have kept us bound for years as mere spectators of a life we believe is possible to experience but which we may also believe we never will do. Also, as we look around us, we may feel that there is no one who could help us remove our grave clothes, no one whom we feel we could trust with the truth of our grave clothes – and so we may feel doubly trapped. Thankfully, even if this is our reality, the Spirit of Christ within us is more than able to guide us in knowing how to deal with our particular grave cloths. We only have to ask.

The following prayer practice may help us to do just that.

Practice: A prayer for release

Every one of us is Lazarus. Every one of us has been called into new life by the powerful, reviving word of Jesus, and, just like Lazarus, every one of us has stepped into that new life wrapped in grave clothes that we may have worn for years. As the Holy Spirit has done his work of unbinding and releasing us, many of us have experienced an undreamed-of freedom. We have experienced release from attitudes, beliefs and behaviours which had kept us tightly bound for years. We know the wonder of being free to live as we always hoped we could; to live with joy and with peace in our relationship with

God and with others. But we know too that there is so much more to experience, that there are still the remnants of grave clothes in our lives which hinder our living fully and freely.

Although Lazarus had human help with his grave clothes, unlike Lazarus, we have the Holy Spirit within us and alongside us to unbind and release us from whatever is restricting our fullest experience of living freely.

Steps into the prayer

It's helpful to engage with this prayer in a place that is undisturbed and quiet, where we can be free to express to God whatever is on our hearts in whatever way we need to, without fear of being interrupted or overheard. It would also be helpful if we could allow enough time not to feel the pressure to rush through the prayer.

The first step in being released from the power of a particular grave cloth is to pray that we would actually recognise and be able to name our cloth. We often don't know what it is that is binding us, what is hindering our fullest experience of Jesus' life in us, so we need the Lord to reveal it to us. So, in the quiet of this moment, place your heart, your mind and your will under the protection of the Holy Spirit, and ask the Spirit to bring to your mind a grave cloth which he may want to release you from. Jesus told us that the Holy Spirit will lead us into all truth (John 16:13), and we can trust that he will do that in these moments; he will bring to our minds the one thing he wants to reveal to us. The very moment we pray this, however, we may experience a barrage of distracting thoughts – 'I need to put the washing on before coffee', 'I wonder whether I sent that email to John'. When those thoughts crowd into that moment, acknowledge them and then just let them go, or make a quick note of them for later, and return to your desire to hear from God the word he wants to speak to you. If it helps to return you to your prayer, you might want to simply pray, 'Speak, Lord, your servant is listening' (from 1 Samuel 3:10).

As the Lord brings to mind the grave cloth he wants to remove, don't be surprised by your response. There may be tears, dismay, anger or anxiety – or a whole range of emotions. Know that you are safe to express to the Lord anything that you may feel at this time; you don't need to censor it or censure it; you are known and loved and accepted. Allow yourself to feel whatever response wells up in you and express that feeling to the Lord.

When you are ready to move on, take some time to think about how that grave cloth became part of your life, how it has influenced your life, how it has shaped the person you are today. Talk through these thoughts with the Lord; bring them all to him, unwrap every detail, pour out to him every emotion surrounding that grave cloth, knowing that there is nothing that you say which will shock, surprise, bother or bore him. Nothing you can say will cause him to withdraw from you; your very need draws him to you as surely as a baby's cry draws the heart of their parent to them.

After some time, you might want to pray this prayer or a similar prayer of your own:

> Father (or whatever name for God is most real for you), I bring to you this grave cloth of _____. It has clung to me for years, preventing me from living as you created and called me to live. I surrender it to you now. In your love and by your power, release me from the control of this grave cloth through any means you may want to use. My heart's desire is to live in the freedom of being a redeemed and beloved child of God. I ask you to answer my prayer in your time and in your way. In Jesus' name. Amen

After you have prayed this prayer, you might want to be quiet for a few moments longer, to remain in God's presence and allow the peace of God to hold your heart and your mind. Notice any further thoughts that you might have – for example, you might sense that the Lord wants you to talk about this grave cloth with someone you trust. You might sense that you need the kind of help Lazarus received as the community around him unwrapped him. The Lord might bring to your mind some practical ideas which he might want to work through with you in order to secure your release.

Whatever comes to your mind during this time, again, just bring those thoughts to the Lord, trusting that he is leading you and will continue to lead you into the freedom that he longs to be yours.

We may pray this prayer many, many times over the years – I know I have – and each time we do, we can rest in knowing that the God of all hope and freedom and grace will welcome us into his presence with all the love of his heart for all the need of our own hearts. He is committed to our fullest freedom. He *will* answer our prayer, but he will do so in his own time and way.

A note of caution

A couple of years ago, the dressing over a surgical wound I had needed to be changed. Rather than bother our busy GP, I choose to do this myself at home with the help of a friend. I had no idea how painful it would be! My friend was gentleness itself as she pulled the dressing away from my skin, but every little tug felt as though my skin was coming off because the dressing's adhesive edges were like superglue. There was no way she could just rip it off, and the whole event took much longer than I imagined it would.

Some of our grave clothes may have been wrapped around our hearts and our minds for so very long that they seem to have become superglued into our very being, and removing them may be painful and take much longer than we would have imagined. The Holy Spirit is a good and kind friend, and, in his wisdom, he may take whatever time is needed to gently peel away our grave clothes. We can be confident, though, that however long it takes, however painful it may be, the wonder of being able to move into our fullest freedom and into the fullest purpose of God's heart for us will be worth it – it really will.

3

Of streams and cisterns and a satisfied heart

'If anyone is thirsty, let him come to me and drink.'
JOHN 7:37 (NLV)

Who does not thirst…?
Hudson Taylor[20]

I expected sand – lots of it: a *Lawrence of Arabia* panorama of sweeping sand dunes, sun-whitened tents and camels. Instead, I got harsh grey rocky terrain: a cratered moonscape of a place, littered with the rusting carcasses of windowless buses. I hadn't expected this part of the Taklamakan Desert to be so bleak, so dreary, so very dusty. My friends and I had travelled for hours through this greyness in the north-west of China, and then suddenly, on the distant horizon, a startling stab of green, which grew and grew as our ancient bus trundled ever nearer on its way into the grape-trellised streets of this, our destination, the oasis city of Turpan.

Exploring the city later that day, we were surprised to see deep troughs of water running alongside the pavements. This water originated from a spring outside the city which had been harnessed and diverted in such an effective way that the city was green and vibrant even in 40-plus degree heat. The only explanation for the surreal sight of the grapevines which canopied the streets of Turpan was the presence of this water, which refreshed and renewed and literally brought life to the people who lived there. The presence of this water completely transformed that desert place – and it's into the same radical transformation that Jesus invites us with these expansive words: 'If anyone is thirsty, let him come to me and drink' (John 7:37, NLV).

The invitation

Throughout the gospels, Jesus employs a variety of metaphors to give us the fullest possible picture of who he is. He refers to himself as bread, light, the way, a gate, a door. All these are helpful metaphors, but here, in this invitation, he identifies himself with the one thing which we cannot live without: water. Just as our bodies need life-sustaining infusions of water to survive, so our souls – the deepest, innermost part of who we are – in order to truly live need to take great gulping draughts of the life of Jesus. In this invitation, Jesus is not offering us helpful advice on how to live life to the full; he is offering himself to us, a consistent and continuous source of life-giving water to refresh and renew our weary souls, to wash away the stain of our sins, to soothe and to cool the pain of our regrets, to bring to life what is dying in us and to sustain what is healthy and growing and life-giving. He offers himself to us as the water that can soften the harder places of our lives, that can quench and satisfy the aching thirsts of our longings and desires.

In this invitation, Jesus is holding out to us nothing less than the hope of a transformed life; the hope that our ordinary everyday lives, infused with the power and the presence of *his* life, can be lived differently in ways we might never have dreamed possible.

The context of the invitation

The circumstances of the lives of those first-century men and women who heard this invitation may have been radically different from our own 21st-century ones, but the deepest needs of our souls are no different, and this becomes clear as we unwrap the context in which this invitation was given.

John introduces this particular invitation of Jesus with the words, 'On the last and greatest day of the Feast' (John 7:37, TLV). I had spent years glancing over this whisper of an introduction, hop-scotching over John's words in my eagerness to get to Jesus' words, but one day, reading these words out loud, I actually heard them, noticed them. I realised I had no understanding of the significance of this particular feast or what explosive impact Jesus' words would have in this specific context. Digging into the commentaries, I discovered that the whole festival was drenched in symbolism which would have been immediately relevant to those who were listening, but which can be lost for us today with our limited understanding of Jewish feasts and festivals.

The feast that John is referring to is the Feast of Tabernacles, which, along with Passover and Pentecost, was one of the big three feasts which all Jewish men were required to attend. All of the feasts were memorials of God's saving actions for his people, each one reminding the people of God's love and commitment to them, of his goodness and care of them. But they were also reminders of the people's need of him as the source and sustainer of their lives; they were tangible, visible reminders of their dependence on him.

This particular feast lasted for eight days and took place in Jerusalem, just after the olive and the grape harvests had been gathered in and before the autumn rains arrived. Because of its timing, it was also known as the Festival of the Ingathering. In many ways, it would have been the equivalent of our own harvest festivals. It was a celebration of God's provision in the present, while at the same time looking forward to the fulfilment of Zechariah's prophesy that one day all nations would be gathered into Jerusalem (Zechariah 14:16). It was also known as the Festival of Booths, commemorating the time when the children of Israel lived in tents as they made their way through the desert to the promised land. During the feast, little booths or shelters made of palm branches were set up on the roof of homes, along the streets and in the fields around Jerusalem. The people ate and prayed in these little booths for the whole of the eight days of the festival, as a reminder of God's protective care and provision for them in the desert. It was also known as the Feast of Joy. During those days, they ate the best foods, drank the best wine and the men danced through the night in bright candlelit exuberance. This feast, of all the feasts, was an incredibly joyful time.

The ceremony

The central symbolic component of this feast was the water-pouring ceremony, which was a stirring reminder of the time when God provided water for the people of Israel during their trek through the desert. At that time, their thirst had been desperate and all-consuming – and God had met that thirst with bubbling fresh water which gushed from the most unexpected of places: a rock. It was an event which demonstrated the power of God and his complete authority and control over all he had created – including water-filled rocks!

Every morning of the feast, the glorious spectacle of this ceremony began with a parade of priests trooping down the rocky road from the temple to the Gihon Spring. They were led by a priest who carried a golden pitcher, which he filled with pure, fresh water from the gurgling spring. As he dipped his pitcher into the water, the assembled people would hear the words of Isaiah 12:3: 'Therefore with joy shall ye draw water out of the wells of salvation' (KJV). Turning, the priests would then walk back up through the crowd-thronged street to the massive altar where the morning sacrifices were laid out.

When they reached the altar, the priest holding the golden pitcher would walk around it once, then lifting the pitcher high enough for everyone to see, he would pour the water into a silver basin on the west side of the altar, where it flowed down through a pipe and into a channel at the base of the altar. At exactly the same time as he did this, another priest would pour wine into a basin on the east side of the altar, where it made its way to the base of the altar to mingle with the water gathering there. The mingled water and wine signified to all who saw it the hope of a life suffused with joy. As this outpouring of water and wine was taking place, 4,000 choir members and 287 instrumentalists burst into exultant song, singing the words of the Hallel Psalms, the mighty praise songs of Psalms 113—118. And then all the people assembled there joined them in singing the words from Psalm 118:25, 'Please, Lord, please save us. Please, Lord, please give us success.' It was a prayer for deliverance, sung with great passion, which allowed the ordinary people to be a part of this great spectacle that was being enacted before them.

On the last day, the priest would perform this same ritual, but this time he would walk round the altar seven times to commemorate the battle of Jericho and how the Lord had opened the way into the promised land, a land flowing with streams of water.

Every aspect of the feast was designed to be a reminder of God's vital presence with his people. The outpoured water was an enactment of God's promise to them in which he declared, 'I will pour water on the thirsty land... my Spirit on your offspring' (Isaiah 44:3, NIV). It pointed forward to the future when the Messiah would come and when the Spirit would be poured out as generously as that water.

But they had been doing this year after year after year – and nothing had changed. The promised Messiah had not come; the Spirit had not been poured out. The best they could hope for was that the autumn rains, on which they were so dependent, would arrive on time and flood the dry ravines and dried-up riverbeds of the land. These men and women were weary with disappointment; they were witnesses to the promise of a life and a destiny which bore no resemblance to the reality of their days and provided no comfort for the broken, dried-up hopes of their own hearts.

The crowd

The men and women who thronged the streets that day were God's people – his own special and chosen ones – and they were in the right place at the right time doing the right thing. Many would have made significant sacrifices to be there for that week: they might have left behind jobs that needed doing and situations and people that needed their attention; they might have left unresolved issues and uncompleted work. They might also have interrupted happy occasions to be at the feast. Whatever was going on in their lives, they had left it all behind and in obedience to God's ordinances had come to this required feast. They were being obedient and sacrificial. And Jesus saw it all: beyond the smiles, he saw the depth of their heartache; beneath the exuberant shouts of the Hallel, he heard the whispered groans of their hearts for true deliverance.

Through the prophet Isaiah, God had declared: 'When the poor and needy search for water and there is none, and their tongues are parched from thirst, then I, the Lord, will answer them. I, the God of Israel, will never abandon them' (Isaiah 41:17). And here he is, Jesus, the good shepherd, who knows with a shepherd's heart that however excited they may be now, these men and women are actually like harassed and helpless, directionless and desperately uncared-for sheep, abandoned by the leaders that God had appointed to care for them (see Ezekiel 34:1–6). So, like the good shepherd he is, he leads his sheep – not to water, but to himself; he calls them to come to him and to receive from him water that will never dry up, will never be less than what they will ever need.

There is a desperate urgency to Jesus' call to them, because he knew that at the end of the festival they would go home to exactly the same lives they'd left behind. They would leave this place, and nothing would be different. They had come to the feast, they had had a good time, they had sung heart-stirring songs, heard good teaching, met up with some friends they hadn't seen since the last feast – and sometime during the last day, they would load up their donkeys, settle their children and make the long journey home.

I wonder if there isn't a poignant similarity here with the experience of some of us who have enjoyed a stimulating time at a conference or a church weekend away. We return home, buoyed for a few hours – or even a few days – with fresh hope that *this* time, our lives really will be different, that *this* time the experience will last, only to find that the reality of our days sucks the life out of our hope and makes a mockery of our dreams of change; dreams of more, dreams of a better song to sing.

These dry-hearted men and women were about to walk away, and Jesus knew that unless they came to him and experienced the life he was so longing to give them, they would go home as thirsty as when they had arrived. So, on that last day of the feast, he called out to them in words that were both evocative and provocative.

The call

The words 'called out' are a very tame translation for what Jesus is doing here! In the original Greek, it is more akin to a shout, a yell, a desperate pleading. The same word is used to describe Bartimaeus shouting out to Jesus for mercy; it is Peter's desperate appeal to Jesus to save him as he sinks; it's the same word used to describe the anguished cry of the Gadarene demoniac as he is faced with the power of the Son of God. This one word tells us that this was no casual invitation, a take-it-or-leave-it offer. This was an aching plea, wrung from the heart of God as he looked through compassionate eyes at the men and women before him, squeezing what little life they could out of the rituals they were witnessing. So he shouts, 'If *anyone is thirsty*, let him come to me and drink...'

In the scriptures, the word 'thirst' is used to describe deep longing and ardent desire. It is also a profound consciousness of need. We hear the psalmists pouring out their longing for God: 'O God… my soul *thirsts* for you; my whole body *longs* for you in this parched and weary land where there is no water' (Psalm 63:1), or 'As the deer longs for streams of water, so I *long* for you, O God. I *thirst* for God, the living God' (Psalm 42:1–2).

What these psalmists seem to recognise, in ways we may barely acknowledge, is that their thirsts were ultimately thirsts for God himself. I wonder how many of us recognise that our nameless, unspoken, deep-buried longings, which every now and then rise to the surface and cry out to be acknowledged, are actually longings for God.

The ways in which our hearts, bodies and minds experience these thirsts are a reflection of our soul's need for God and for what only God can be and can do for us, but we have become so expert at attending to and satisfying the immediate demands of our thirsts with temporary fixes that we can hardly recognise their true nature any more. The immediate has masked an eternal truth – that our hearts were shaped to be filled and satisfied by the God who created those hearts in his image, and who alone can satisfy our deepest needs.

Created in the image of the God who is love, our hearts yearn for love; we yearn to be seen and known, to be appreciated and understood, to be celebrated and enjoyed. Created in the image of a purposeful God, we long for our lives to have purpose and meaning; we long for significance and contribution, to know that our lives make a difference in our world. We long for the acknowledgement of our gifts and strengths and for a place in which they can be fulfilled and satisfied. And being created in the image of the God who is creator, we long to express the creativity that is inherent in our lives in ways that bring joy and life to others, even as we experience joy and life in the act of creating. All of our thirsts can be traced back, eventually, to our creation in the image of God, and we thrive in every fibre of our being when those thirsts are met and fulfilled by the God who alone can satisfy them.

The wonder of this invitation is its expansiveness and inclusiveness; Jesus does not specify or quantify the thirst. There are no restrictions here. His call, 'Come to me!', is to *anyone* who is aware of deep longings in their lives, aware that life as they know it is not all they thought it could be and hoped it would be, and who long for more, even if they have no clue what that 'more' is or could possibly look like.

At a time of devastating bereavement, Hudson Taylor, a pioneer missionary in the 19th century, wrote, 'Who does not thirst? Who has not mind-thirsts or heart-thirsts, soul-thirsts or body-thirsts? Well, no matter which, or whether I have them all, "Come unto ME" and remain thirsty? Ah, no! "Come unto ME and drink."'[21]

Taylor poignantly captures this generous expansiveness in Jesus' invitation to come and drink. It is, in essence, a blank cheque to be filled in with the name of our thirsts; whatever the nature of our thirsts, whatever their history, their depths, the places they have led us to in our attempts to satisfy them, Jesus invites us to come to him, to bring the blank cheque of our needs to him without shame or guilt or fear that we will be turned away or that we will leave more empty than we came. As we come to him in the jumble of our neediness., we step into a loving, compassionate welcome; an assurance that there is no shame in our longings, not here. We have come to the right place – the only place – where the depths of our thirsts can be met by the depths of a longing to satisfy them.

An act of trust

But what does coming to Jesus and drinking actually look like? Perhaps the first thing to note is that this is not a one-time event.

The verb tense of the Greek words used for 'come' and for 'drink' here implies a continuous action: to come and to keep on coming, to drink and to keep on drinking. It reminds me of seeing the runners in the London Marathon who kept sipping from their water bottles throughout the course of the race. However large a gulp they took at the beginning of the race, it would not be enough to sustain them through the whole race – so they kept sipping until the race was over. Many of us hope that a good sermon on a Sunday, or attending a mid-week home group, will be enough to keep us spiritually hydrated through the week – but it's not enough. Just as we need to keep physically hydrated throughout our days, so we need to come daily to Jesus to receive from him the life-sustaining water that our souls need in order to be satisfied.

The act of drinking is intentional and deliberate. In the same way as we open our mouths to drink, drinking here means that in our times with Jesus, we open up to him our needs and our desires, we open up to him the reality of our lives. And just as the act of drinking requires us to swallow, so coming to Jesus and drinking from him requires an act of trust. Immediately following his invitation to drink, Jesus states, 'Whoever *believes* in me…' In the original Greek, 'drink' and 'believe' are what is known as paired words, leading us to understand that in this context, drinking and believing are one act. But this word 'believe' is not a cold, abstract word; it's not a book-based academic acknowledgement of a fact; it's deeply personal and relational. It's wrapped up in having confidence enough in someone to entrust ourselves to them, heart and soul. It means to trust – and to keep on trusting.

In this compelling invitation, Jesus is inviting us to trust him, to trust that what we read about him in the Bible is actually true. So when we read that he is our shepherd, we trust him to guide us when we have no clue where we are going or how to get there. When we read that Jesus is kind and full of mercy, we trust him with the full details of our sin, with the messes of our lives, with our regrets and our shame. When we read that Jesus wept, we trust him with those things that are breaking our own hearts. We not only believe in our heads that what we read of Jesus is true, but we take the risk that it can be true *for us* – and we act on it.

Like any invitation that lands on our doormat, Jesus' invitations to trust come in different-sized, different-shaped 'envelopes'. Sometimes our invitation arrives in an envelope which may take the shape and size of an unexpected financial demand which leaves us with little left. Sometimes it is the envelope of a confidence betrayed, a disappointed hope or a broken dream. Sometimes the invitation to trust comes in an envelope shaped by a sense of God's absence and a longing for his presence. Sometimes the envelope is a large one – it arrives as a long-term illness or an unrelenting demand on our lives which we are forced to live with day in and day out. But sometimes it's the envelope of a new and exciting opportunity, a chance to step out of the boat of our security and to venture into the deep, to take a risk. Whatever the shape, colour or size of the envelope, when we open it, we discover the words of an invitation addressed to us, personally: 'My beloved child, will you trust me in this? Your loving Father, Abba.'

Some years ago I received an invitation to trust which came in the envelope of a new role which was exciting and attractive, but which would entail a great deal more responsibility. And I was scared – scared of failing and being seen to fail. I was scared too of falling flat on my face and fearful of disappointing the expectations of those who offered me the role. I was keenly aware that this new role would not only give me wonderful opportunities to use my gifts and my strengths and my experience, but also expose my weaknesses and vulnerabilities – and there would be nowhere to hide.

Walking helps me to pray, so walking around the streets of my neighbourhood one evening, I poured out to the Lord all the fears that this invitation stirred up in me. I piled word upon word until I felt I'd said everything there was to say and then I stopped. In the silence that followed, I sensed the Lord's response within my heart –

simple and gracious: 'If you fail, we'll figure out together what you need to do next.' That was all. No assurance that I would not fail, but the assurance that if I did fail, I would not be alone to figure out what to do next. The Lord promised his help, and in that moment it was enough.

But the moment passed so quickly! Tripping unceremoniously over a loose paving stone prompted more prayer, this time over my fear of falling. I'm not sure I understood what I meant by 'falling' – and all these years later as I recall that moment, I'm still not too sure – but the wonder of the kind wisdom of God is that he is able to hear past our incomprehensible mutterings to the fear and the doubt and the distress which birth our words. Naomi Levy writes that 'God knows our deepest thoughts and our deepest hurts. We don't have to explain. We don't even have to say a single word.'[22] Our wordless sighs are heard and understood and taken seriously.

Clumsily unwrapping this particular fear in God's presence, I sensed God assuring me, 'If you fall, I'll catch you!' The highly graphic description that I had painted of what falling might look like for me was met with the words of Deuteronomy 33:27, a verse I'd memorised years before and which now flooded my fear-soaked mind: 'The eternal God is your dwelling place and *underneath are the everlasting arms*' (ESV). I might fall, but I could only fall into the arms of God! I could never fall lower than those arms because, however far I fell, however hard I fell, his arms were always lower, always underneath me, strong and tender. There was nowhere to go where he would not already be present, and he would be there with all of the grace and kindness and resources and support that I would need. A few days later, I took a deep breath of trust and accepted the invitation and took on a role which I held with joy and thankfulness for the next 15 years.

I had come to him with my need, and he had met my need with the promise of his presence and the assurance of his grace-filled involvement with me. It was a strong trust-building moment in my relationship with the Lord, and one which seemed to confirm for me a truth I was slowly coming to recognise: that I'm not sure we ever really experience the depth of who Jesus can be for us until we come to him barefaced and naked in our need, stripped of all posturing and pretence, and allow him to clothe us and cover us with a God-given courage and confidence right there, in that place of neediness. The Lord had given me no assurance of success, just the assurance of his presence with me regardless of how well or how badly things might turn out.

I wonder if we need to acknowledge the truth that Jesus being present and involved in our lives does not mean that every problem gets fixed, every wounded relationship healed, every project blessed with success – as much as we might want it or expect it. What it does mean is that his presence will imbue us with strength and hope to live in that very place free from the grip of fear and crippling dread, and with the confidence to move forwards into whatever we need to do next.

A hydrated soul

Jesus announced to the crowds that day that those who opened their needy hearts to him in trust would experience the wonder of his own life flowing through them by his Spirit, saturating the dry soil of their hearts. Their trust would trigger the flow of his life and power in them and through them. There have been many differing understandings of Jesus' words, 'Rivers of living water will flow from his heart' – but one thing is clearly understood: the life of Jesus flowing through the channels of our own lives will bring about deep transformation in us, the kind of transformation which was illustrated by the presence of water in the city of Turpan. There was a freshness about the city, a vibrancy. In stark contrast with the desert around it, there was colour, lush grapes and refreshing air. The people still had problems and needs, but they didn't live in fear of the water drying up; they had enough experience to trust that the water would always be there, flowing out of that spring. It freed them to live without fear of scarcity or want. They lived with a grateful awareness of the gift of that water, and they seemed to really enjoy life – if the way they danced was anything to go by! Paul writes that we are to live our lives 'not in a dogged religious plod, but in a living, spirited dance' (1 Thessalonians 4:1, MSG). Attending a cultural concert in the city one evening, I saw professional dancers perform with an exuberance that was a living picture of Paul's words here – they danced with a joy and an abandon that was contagious and which drew us into the dance with them.

What that never-ceasing spring of fresh water did for the city of Turpan is what Jesus longs to do for our lives, as the refreshing presence of his life fills and overflows the deep channels of our hearts' needs.

Soul dehydration

The city of Turpan is a lively metaphor for what a hydrated soul may look like, but how do we recognise when our souls are becoming dehydrated? What are the warning signs that we are not just feeling out of sorts, not just experiencing a blip in our experience of God and life, but that there is something going on in the very depths of us to which we need to pay attention – a stagnation in the waters of our souls which demands that we take it seriously?

We can recognise physical dehydration fairly easily – a dry mouth is a helpful warning signal to our bodies that we need water. But that's just the first sign. Along with a dry mouth there are other signals: light-headedness, muscle cramps, dizziness and fatigue. These signals increase in intensity and become more exacerbated with each degree of dehydration.

Physical dehydration is health-destroying, and if it goes on long enough it is life-threatening. But equally threatening to our lives is *spiritual dehydration*. It seems that God has created our souls in such a way that they also have a number of different signals to grab our attention.

Our dehydrated soul may signal itself in physical ways: restless sleep or no sleep at all; a loss of appetite or a craving for food; drinking more alcohol than normal; watching more TV than we usually do. Emotionally, we may erupt into sudden and uncontrollable anger or dissolve in unexpected tears. We may feel crushed by the weight of our anxieties and fears – especially at three in the morning. Spiritually, we may feel more susceptible to certain temptations, and spiritual practices which have always been sustaining may now seem more draining and demanding than life-giving. More generally, there may be a kind of staleness about life and living that seems to linger in a different way than the usual ebb and flow of our emotions over the course of a few weeks. And even though we may be functioning just fine in our roles and responsibilities, these warning lights are there, alerting us to the fact that our souls are drying up.

The problem is that we can be aware of these things in our lives, but not recognise them as signs of a dangerously dehydrating soul – and when we don't recognise the signs for what they truly are, we try to alleviate the symptoms. It's like trying to get rid of the flashing oil can on the instrument panel of your car by driving faster or in a different direction. I actually did that once, and the result was that my engine exploded. The engine and the car were a write-off. I was a new driver and thought I could outrun the oil can. But I learnt a significant life lesson in that situation: *You can't outrun the oil can!*

Broken cisterns

But some of us try. We become like the Israelites of old who, when they became aware of the dryness of their lives, dealt with it not by turning to God, the spring of living water, but by building broken cisterns that could never satisfy their deep needs (Jeremiah 2:13). Fearful that God may actually not be enough to satisfy our deepest needs, we build our own 'broken cisterns'. We may pour ourselves into activities and projects that fill our time but not our hearts. We may indulge in 'soft' addictions: hours spent in front of the television, on the internet or on social media. We may shop till we drop or exercise until we really do drop. We may bury ourselves in our jobs or in an absorbing hobby which gives us satisfaction and some measure of joy. We may spend hours in church-related activities, a constant presence at every event, the volunteer no project can do without. None of these things are wrong in themselves, but when they are used as a means of trying to soothe the ache of our dry and thirsty souls, we need to be aware that something is wrong. We need to recognise them as the warning signals they are and allow them to lead us back to Jesus and to his ever-present invitation to drink.

Pain-proofed hearts

Some of us may be like the Israelites in our attempts to *do* something, anything, to handle our dehydrating souls, but some of us take a different route, a much less obvious way. Rather than looking to things outside of us to satisfy our needs, we bring those needs inside, deadening our longings and desires to such an extent that, eventually, they don't hurt anymore. We pain-proof our hearts, ensuring that our thirsts are no longer a threat to us, convincing ourselves that in the grand scheme of things, they no longer matter.

In this regard, we can resemble an organism called the Arizona roundworm, which has a spectacular way of dealing with the threat of dehydration. This organism shuts itself down and achieves a state known as anhydrobiosis. In order to survive in the extreme summer heat of the Arizona desert, when there is no let-up in the rising air pressure and barely a trace of moisture in the air, the round worm shuts down its main organs, uses 25% of its body mass to protect the vital organs, reduces itself in size, becomes calcified and hunkers down for the duration of the threat to its existence. Its metabolism slows down to such an extent that some scientists wonder whether this roundworm can even be described as alive during this time. But it *is* alive; it's just not living.

Some of us may become emotionally and spiritually anhydrobiotic. We may feel that the needs of our hearts are so deep, the chance of those needs ever being met so impossible, that rather than even attempt to address them ourselves, we shut them down. We may build a protective wall of feigned indifference or disregard around our hearts, and, like the Arizona roundworm, we are alive, but not really living the kind of vibrant, rich life which Jesus describes in John 10:10. We may no longer feel the hurt of our longings, but we are now in danger of being deadened to anything that is good and life-giving for us. In some ways it might be the spiritual equivalent of leprosy – as the disease advances, the leper doesn't feel the pain of a splintered shard of glass, but neither do they feel the silky softness of a baby's hair. It is a sad exchange – but it doesn't need to be this way.

Some years ago I came across these words, written by A.W. Tozer, the great evangelical mystic of the mid 20th century:

> God is so vastly wonderful, so utterly and completely delightful, that he can without anything other than himself meet and overflow the deepest demands of our total nature, mysterious and deep as that nature is.[23]

This is a truth on which we can lean our hearts and our heads. This is the truth which Jesus was holding out to a dry and thirsty, needy and hope-laden people that day in Jerusalem. It is the truth which he holds out to us today. As we embrace this truth for ourselves, we will find not only life and energy flowing *in* us, but also *through* us and out into the lives of others, bringing the life and the power of Jesus into the dry and needy places of our world in ways that are transformative and life-sustaining, refreshing and releasing.

Reflection: Recognising our thirsts, trusting our God

Look over the following areas for reflection, focusing on the one to which you are particularly drawn at this time; you may want to come back to the other areas at a different time.

On transformation

The following quotation is taken from the beginning of the chapter:

> Jesus… is offering himself to us, a consistent and continuous source of life-giving water to refresh and renew our weary souls, to wash away the stain of our sins, to soothe and to cool the pain of our regrets, to bring to life what is dying in us and to sustain what is healthy and growing and life-giving. He offers himself to us as the water that can soften the harder places of our lives, that can quench and satisfy the aching thirsts of our longings and desires.

- Take a moment to reflect and to name those dry and thirsty areas of your life, areas of weariness, regret, hardness, longing or other areas which need the transforming water of the presence of Jesus.
- What transformation would you most long to see in those areas? What difference could you imagine it could make to your life, your relationships, your work, your service to God, to be transformed in those areas? Be as specific as you can be.
- Write a prayer to the Lord expressing your desire for transformation in those particular areas.

The invitation to trust

- Is there an area of your life where you sense that God is inviting you to trust him? For example, your relationships and the various roles you play, your work life, your family, your finances, your personal needs and their fulfilment, your fears and anxieties or sins and regrets.
- What do you sense would be involved in trusting God with this area of your life?
- David in Psalm 62:8 encourages us to 'trust in [God] at all times. Pour out your heart to him.' Take some time now to pour out your heart to the Lord, knowing that you can trust him with everything that is poured out, understanding, as David also testifies, that 'God is our safe place' (Psalm 46:1, NLV).

On broken cisterns and walled-up hearts

'My people have committed two sins: They have forsaken me, the spring of living water, and have dug their own cisterns, broken cisterns that cannot hold water.'

JEREMIAH 2:13 (NIV)

- Do you have a DIY strategy for dealing with your thirsts – a broken cistern of choice or an anhydrobiotic protectiveness?
- As you reflect on that particular strategy, in what ways do you sense it may have drawn you away from trusting Jesus to satisfy your thirst?
- Confess to the Lord the ways in which your own strategies for handling your thirsts have taken you away from him. Express your desire for his help in replacing those strategies with an intentional trust in his love and wise purposes for your life.

4

This is my desire

Lord, all my desire is before You; And my sighing is not hidden from You.

PSALM 38:9 (AMP)

Desire lies at the very heart of what it is to be human. There is an energy within all of us that haunts us and can either lead us to set out on a quest for something more or frustrate us with nostalgia for what we do not have.[24]

Tidings of joy?

They come tucked into Christmas cards which portray shepherds and kings and robins and Cotswold villages sprinkled in glitter-snow; they are *the Christmas newsletter*. Filled with photos of happy families, of holidays taken in increasingly exotic places, of children and grandchildren, of graduation photos ranging from kindergarten to Cambridge, they announce glad tidings of great joy – engagements and marriages, new babies, new jobs and new homes. And in countless homes across the country, men and women who night after night eat their dinner alone, families on benefits who can only dream of a day at Legoland and parents of children whose special needs deprive them of the ordinary life most of us take for granted wonder where they went wrong. They wonder why the desire of their hearts for the life that others write about so easily doesn't seem to have touched God's heart. For most of us, these letters are a delight to receive, a wonderful way of catching up with long-distance friends and relatives. But for many, they serve as reminders of a life that has been longed for, of desires which rub raw the tender edges of our hearts.

Where do our longings and our desires come from? What part do our desires play in shaping our lives and the way we live them? How do we live with our desires in a way that is healthy and life-giving, and how do we recognise when our desires are becoming distorted and life-diminishing? These are important questions for us to consider when we are reflecting on the reasons underlying the draw of a better song to sing, of a different way of living. I wonder whether the beginning of an answer to these questions lies in the place where every desire was good and godly and fulfilled – the garden of Eden.

Genesis 2:8 states: 'The Lord God planted a garden in Eden.' The name 'Eden' means 'delight', and God created it to be just that. This is the place God intended for us to call home – a place of beauty, joy, freedom and intimacy with God and with each other; a place where every desire was good and healthy because it came from hearts that were perfectly aligned with the desires of God. God wanted a world, so he created one – a world of great beauty and diversity. He wanted to populate that world, so created animals and fish and birds, everything from butterflies to buffalos. But God wanted more; the Triune God declared, 'Let us make human beings in our image, to be like us… So God created human beings in his own image' (Genesis 1:26–27). God wanted to share his life, to open up the circle of his love and the doors of his heart – so he did just that! Adam and Eve were created in the image of God, and that God was a God of passionate desire. Our desires mark our creation in the image of God; they are part of our created humanity.

Philip Sheldrake suggests that 'desire lies at the very heart of what it is to be human. There is an energy within all of us that haunts us and can either lead us to set out on a quest for something more or frustrate us with nostalgia for what we do not have.'[25] Eden may be long gone, but in all of us there is something, a trace memory perhaps, which is given substance in the reality of our desires, in the nameless ache we sometimes feel in the beauty of a spectacular sunset or in the soaring notes of a piece of music which bring us to tears. It seems that as natural as it is for a baby to crave milk, there are some desires which seem to be hardwired into our humanity.

Because of the relational intimacy for which we were created, we desire satisfying and fulfilling relationships of all sorts. If single, most of us have a desire to be married; if married, we desire the richest marriage possible; we may desire children and that those children grow and thrive and blossom into all that they could ever be. In our place of work, we may desire supportive and productive relationships with our colleagues. Wherever we 'do life' – family, friendships, workplace, church, leisure activities, social involvement – we want our relationships to be honest and honouring, good-natured and peaceful, open and safe – just as they were in Eden.

We seem to have an innate desire to create, to contribute, to live with purpose, to make a difference in whatever world we inhabit. We want to use our gifts, strengths and abilities in ways that bring out the best in us and that allow us to give our best to others. And then there are the desires of our bodies: we want to live well and to be healthy; to be physically able to do all that we are capable of, to live our lives as well as we can for as long as we can.

We desire integrity in our faith journey too: a deeper understanding of truth, a more intimate relationship with Jesus. Our hearts resonate with the psalmist's yearning: 'The one thing I want from God, the thing I seek most of all, is the privilege of meditating in his Temple, living in his presence every day of my life, delighting in his incomparable perfections and glory' (Psalm 27:4, TLB). We want to experience the fullest dimensions of who God is in our daily lives – to know God as our shepherd, our shield, our very life. We want to know the soul-deep truth of being delighted in by God, being affirmed as the beloved of his heart and being a joy to him. We don't just want to read about this kind of life; we want to live it for ourselves.

When Jesus interacted with the men and women he encountered, he seemed to consistently hone in on their desires. Jesus recognised that so much of the transformation we desire to see in our lives begins with an acknowledgement and an understanding of our God-created desires. So he taught about desire, and he aroused desire through parables which speak of an extravagantly gracious father (Luke 15:11–32), of a super-generous banquet host (Luke 14:15–24) and of a lost coin found by a desperately seeking housewife (Luke 15:8–10). And he asked questions which brushed aside niceties and drew people into facing the real desires of their hearts.

What do you *want*?

In John's gospel, the very first words spoken by Jesus frame a question about desire. Jesus had noticed two men following him, disciples of John the Baptist, so he asked them, 'What do you *want*?' (John 1:38). They answered with a question of their own: 'Where are you staying?' Recognising that these men were not asking for his address but were initiating the possibility of a relationship, Jesus simply said, 'Come and see' (v. 39). It was an invitation to be with him. Those two men spent the rest of the day with Jesus, and for one of them, Andrew, that time resulted in a complete change of life. He eventually left his job as a fisherman and became one of the twelve apostles. Tradition has it that he became a missionary with a wide-ranging ministry whose scope included both modern-day Russia and Greece.

Later in John's gospel we read the account of an encounter which Jesus had with a crippled man who had been lying by the pool of Bethesda for 38 years and who had never been able to get into the healing waters in time to be healed. Jesus asked a very simple question – 'Do you *want* to be healed?' (John 5:6, ESV). It would seem like a no-brainer! Why would he have been lying by the pool for all of those years if he didn't want to get healed? Many people might have asked *why* he hadn't been able to get into the pool, or *why* he hadn't arranged for someone to help him – but Jesus asked a far more penetrating question – 'Do you *want* to get well? Is that really your desire?' It was a kind and heart-searching question. Jesus knew that this man's identity was bound up with his infirmity; his community had been created from those who had gathered around this pool for years. This place was his life: the mat he lay on, his place in that life. But in the silence which followed Jesus' question this man seemed to dig deep, and when Jesus told him to pick up his mat and walk away – he did just that. Jesus' question pushed him to the very edge of his hope, his desire, and somewhere in the depths of his heart he seemed to rediscover it – and responded. In that one trust-filled moment, his life was changed.

In Mark's gospel we encounter the irrepressible Bartimaeus (Mark 10:46–52). We know nothing of this man except that he was blind and a beggar. His begging spot that day was on the busy road which led out of Jericho and on to Jerusalem. Sitting there, he picked up the news that Jesus was passing by. He had obviously heard of Jesus and his ministry and, although he may have been blind, he was not deaf or mute. Sensing a change in the tone of the crowd as Jesus approached, he yelled out to Jesus, 'Son of David, have mercy on me.' He was immediately shushed by his superiors – which basically meant everyone! He was blind and a beggar; they didn't come much lower on the social and religious ladder of those days. He could go no lower, so instead he reached up with the only thing he had – his loud voice – and he yelled out to Jesus, and Jesus heard the yearning in that yell and called him over.

'What do you *want* me to do for you?' Jesus asked him (Mark 10:51). I wonder if Bartimaeus had ever been asked that question before. I wonder if any kind person had ever asked how they could help him. We'll never know, but what we do know is that when Jesus asked him, he was ready with his answer: 'I want to see.' I wonder again how many, many times he had muttered those words to himself as he wrapped himself in his cloak at night. I wonder how many times he had wept over the fact of his blindness and all the ways that his blindness had shaped and limited his life. But in a heartbeat, all that was changed. With a word, Jesus brought healing – and this beggar's life was changed. The first face he would see would be the face of the incarnate God; the first eyes he looked into would be eyes that shone with the love and the compassion and the kindness of God for *him*, Bartimaeus. Jesus gave him back his life – and Bartimaeus picked up that life and, without a backward glance, left his beggar's bowl and his cloak behind and followed Jesus on the road to Jerusalem.

As these cameos illustrate, our desires, recognised, owned and expressed before God, open up the possibility of transformation in our lives, of deep and lasting change, of a different way of living. Even owning up to God our desire to eat a whole box of chocolates in one sitting is not as shallow a desire as it may originally seem, because as we engage with God about this, working down from that surface desire, we may eventually get to the need and the longing underlying the desire for chocolate. We may discover that indulging this particular desire is not actually a joy, but an act of resignation. We may be so dissatisfied with ourselves and with the way our lives are going, so aware of our restless yearning for more – in our jobs, our relationships, our walk with God – that chocolate in all its glory is our place of sure and certain comfort. (I know this from experience!) As we bring this seemingly superficial desire to God, we open ourselves up to anything and everything that his good heart would want for us.

But there are deeper desires too, and if we allow God to sift through them, he may reveal to us that there is far more to our desires than we might ever have known or understood. Our desire for marriage, for example, may reveal a fear of aloneness, a longing to belong, to be special to someone, anyone; it may actually be a desire to be known and understood and seen for who we really are, a desire for acceptance, for affirmation. When we feel that this desire is not being met in one relationship, we may move on to another, trusting that the next one will be 'the one'. Unless we allow God to be the one who mirrors our desirability and worth and wonder, we may find ourselves moving from one person to another, always looking, always disappointed, always wanting more.

For some of us, our desire for perfection in every aspect of our lives may be uncovered as a fiercely protective effort to ensure that nothing has the chance to go wrong in our lives. Perfection can mask our fear of being seen as the frail and fallible human being we know we are. We may believe that if we can only live a perfect life in our homes, our workplaces, in all the places where we feel our presence matters, then there will never be a reason for anyone to reject us or exclude us or consider us to be less than the image we have worked so hard to portray. We need to know that God alone is perfect – and that he does not demand perfection from us. Knowing that our acceptance is not based on our performance can help us to rest in who we were created to be, to accept our mistakes and our limitations as being part of what it means to be human.

Our keen desire for social justice, for an end to conflict, for righteous government, is an honourable desire which reflects the heart of a God who is more passionate about these issues than we could ever be. God declared this passion through prophets like Amos, who recorded God's longing that justice would 'roll on like a river, righteousness like a never-failing stream!' (Amos 5:24, NIV). But our God-reflecting, passionate convictions may need to be surrendered into a deeper and broader wisdom than our own. Job expressed it well when he said, 'Indeed these are the mere edges of His ways, And how small a whisper we hear of Him!' (Job 26:14, NKJV). We can only see a tiny sliver of the world and how it is working – whereas God sees it all, for time and eternity, and will continue to pursue his purposes to bring justice to the nations without panic or dread.

But the truth is that many of us can be leery of our desires, our longings, our yearnings, perhaps fearful that they are so deeply unholy that they are unworthy of being expressed to a holy God. Consequently they remain buried under layers of guilt and fear and the heavy weight of accumulated disappointments. Many of us are convinced that our desires are basically bad (or God would have fulfilled them), and so, being bad, they need to be corralled somewhere safe – for example, in the structure of a rigidly disciplined and ascetic life – or they will run amok and ruin our lives. Or we've taken a risk and a deep breath and we've poured out our desires to God – our unfulfilled desires have worn out the knees of our prayers – but God has not responded, at least in any way that we recognise as a response. So where do we go with our unfulfilled desires, and how do we live with our desires in a way that honours God and honours too the transforming power inherent in those desires?

Living with our desires

There seem to be at least three major options available to us as we face living with our desires:

- indulge them
- deny or disown them
- acknowledge them and direct them towards God in trust and surrender.

Indulge them

'Whatever my eyes desired I did not keep from them; I kept my heart from no pleasure' (Ecclesiastes 2:10, NRSV). This was Solomon's testimony, and thousands of years later our own culture seems to reflect Solomon's attitude to desire – although we may not be as honest as he was in stating the outcome: 'It was all so meaningless – like chasing the wind' (v. 11). We live in a culture which seems to encourage us to indulge our every desire; if you see it, if you want it, it can be yours – for the right price. Advertisers know a million and one ways to hook into our desires, convincing us that we need more and better and different than what we already have in order to be satisfied. Sadly, and perhaps not unsurprisingly, the cost is usually much higher than we ever thought we would pay. Indulging our every whim may lock us into a relentless pursuit of satisfaction, which eventually spirals downwards into a chasm of unsatisfied longing, a drivenness which is ultimately destructive. Our hearts were never created to be satisfied by things or experiences, and if we surrender ourselves into the arms of our indulgences, we may slowly but surely lose our capacity for joy, for pleasure and for life itself.

Deny or disown them

In contrast to the commercial pressure of the world, the teaching which many of us have received in our churches has been heavy on resisting this cultural influence. Rather than being taught how to handle our desires in a healthy, God-honouring, life-affirming way, many of us have been taught to distrust, deny or disown our desires.

We may have been taught that our desires originate in our hearts and that our hearts are 'deceitful above all things, and desperately wicked' (Jeremiah 17:9, KJV). Whatever is born of such a heart is therefore itself deceitful, wicked and not to be trusted.

I remember as a young believer being so confused by this teaching. I was encouraged to ask Jesus into my heart in order to experience his gift of new life, and when I did, I was asked, 'Where is Jesus now?' The answer, 'In my heart', was affirmed and delighted in. 'You ask me how I know he lives, he lives within my heart,' I sang with gusto and with deep thankfulness. Jesus was in my heart; God himself had taken up residence in my heart by his Spirit. How amazing was that? I had the mind of Christ (1 Corinthians 2:16); I had Jesus living in my heart – and yet my heart was still wicked? My heart was still a source of evil? How could that be? I was confused.

When we have been taught that, although redeemed, the true nature of our heart is wicked and deceitful, then it is natural that if we want to be wholehearted followers of Jesus we will deny the desires of our hearts any room in our lives. We will dismiss them as foolishness at best and wickedness at worst. In addition, when the teaching we have received has also been heavy on sacrifice or self-denial for the sake of Christ, we may be deeply ashamed of our desires, condemning them as selfishly ungodly and ourselves as unworthy of the life and death of Jesus.

Sadly, out of a deep unease at the legitimacy of our desires, or fear of the strength of our desires and the chaos they may cause in our lives if we were ever to pursue them, we may cauterise our desires and, in doing so, may harm ourselves. In Jesus' day there was a type of Pharisee called the Blind, Bruised or Bleeding Pharisee; these God-fearing men were so fearful of lustful desires being aroused when they saw a beautiful woman coming towards them that they would shut their eyes. Naturally, they bumped into posts, people or obstacles in their paths, which left them bruised and bleeding! Foolish, perhaps, but I wonder how many of us live with bruised and bleeding hearts because we have been so afraid that our desires will completely overwhelm us and lead us astray that we have deliberately shut our eyes to whatever it is we may desire, and deafened our hearts to the whispers that our desires may be good and even God-given. I wonder if the blanketing numbness which we may sometimes experience as we go through our days is caused by the dragging weight of our disowned desires, clinging desperately to the hem of our hearts. It takes real courage to feed our hungry hearts with hope, yet that is the only real solution to holding our desires in a healthy way: to hope, and to continue to hope, as we surrender our hearts to God until the burden of that hopefulness is lifted – one way or another.

This is not to deny the truth that our desires may become distorted into something which actually robs us of life; there is no doubt that a good and healthy desire may morph into something unhealthy, which we need to be aware of: a demand that God come through for us – that he honours our desires – in the ways in which we want them honoured.

Direct our desires towards God

If we are not to indulge, deny, dismiss or disown our desires, what are we to do with them?

It seems that the healthiest way to handle our desires is to acknowledge them, to name them and own them, to bring them to God in prayer, surrendering them to his love, wisdom and goodness in trust and confidence that he knows all there is to know of those desires and he cares. The psalmist wrote, 'You know what I long for, Lord; you hear my every sigh' (Psalm 38:9). And this is true for us, too. Every single dimension of our desires is known to God, even if we ourselves barely understand them.

1 Samuel 1 gives us a beautiful insight into how one woman brought her desire to God. In the early verses of this chapter we are introduced to Hannah, a woman who was unable to conceive in a culture where a woman's worth and dignity was bound up in her fertility. Hannah's grief over her condition was exacerbated by having to spend her days in the company of an obviously fertile woman, Peninnah, her husband's other wife. Hannah's longing for a child, and Peninnah's taunting and mocking of her childlessness, continued year after year (v. 7). But what is so amazing about Hannah is that she didn't give up her hope that God would one day listen to her desperate plea and answer it with a child. The Bible records for us the prayer of this broken woman:

> Once when they had finished eating and drinking in Shiloh, Hannah stood up. Now Eli the priest was sitting on his chair by the doorpost of the Lord's house. In her deep anguish Hannah prayed to the Lord, weeping bitterly. And she made a vow, saying, 'Lord Almighty, if you will only look on your servant's misery and remember me, and not forget your servant but give her a son, then I will give him to the Lord for all the days of his life, and no razor will ever be used on his head.'
> 1 SAMUEL 1:9–11 (NIV)

Her distress and her anguish drove her to pour out her heart to the God she acknowledges as the Lord Almighty, the all-powerful ruler over the entire universe, the one who holds all power and authority in his hands. This is the God she addresses, the God she honours as mighty and powerful, able to do whatever he desires. And she approaches this God as his servant. Twice she identifies herself as 'servant': not a term of entitlement, but a term of dependence and humility. She makes no demand, but she does make a promise – to give her son to the Lord 'all the days of his life'. Because the family were Levites, her son would have belonged to the Lord anyway as his servant, but the Levites only served from the age of 30–50 and then they were free. Here, Hannah is promising this son to the Lord for all the days of his life. She is gifting her son to the Lord.

Eli the priest had watched Hannah at prayer, and although initially scolding her for being drunk, he believed Hannah when she told him that she had been pouring out her heart to the Lord, praying to him in great anguish and sorrow (vv. 15–16). So he blessed her, saying, 'May the God of Israel grant the request you have asked of him' (v. 17), and Hannah went home 'and she was no longer sad' (v. 18). She believed the blessing; she was already joyful and worshipping before she ever conceived. She believed God had heard her desperate plea, and she lived out of that faith in confidence and in a happy anticipation of what was to come.

Her experience puts flesh on the bones of Paul's words in Philippians 4:6–7: 'Don't worry about anything; instead, pray about everything. Tell God what you need, and thank him for all he has done. Then you will experience God's peace, which exceeds anything we can understand. His peace will guard your hearts and minds as you live in Christ Jesus.' Paul doesn't say that the peace comes after the prayer has been answered! The peace comes after we have poured out the desires, longings and needs of our hearts to God, trusting him to answer out of his love of us, his good heart towards us and his complete knowledge of our place in the unfolding of the purposes of his heart.

Paula Rinehart comments that Hannah is 'a beautiful mixture of relentless hope and a surrendered heart',[26] and as such she is a good model for us in acknowledging our desires, owning them and specifically naming them before God – and believing that the God who can do all things will do for us everything that is needed for our best. God sees the end from the beginning. He knows where our un-surrendered desires may lead us, but he knows too the time and the way in which our desires may be satisfied to the full and for our best.

Knowing God: our deepest desire

In reflecting on the nature of our desires, C.S. Lewis concludes:

> It would seem that our Lord finds our desires not too strong, but too weak. We are half-hearted creatures, fooling about with drink and sex and ambition when infinite joy is offered us, like an ignorant child who wants to go on making mud pies in a slum because he cannot imagine what is meant by the offer of a holiday at the sea. We are far too easily pleased.[27]

Perhaps one of the reasons why God allows us to desire so much for so long is to bring us to the place, eventually, where having sifted our desires through the sieve of time and tears, we discover to our surprise that our deepest desire really is to know him. Perhaps there are other times when God does answer the prayers of our hearts so that in receiving what we desire, we discover that although 'a desire fulfilled is sweet to the soul' (Proverbs 13:19, ESV), that sweetness actually isn't enough to satisfy and bring peace to the depths of our souls. We thought it would be; we thought the new house, the latest smart phone, the next promotion, the relationship we'd longed for would soothe the hungry desires of our hearts, but over time we discover the truth that our hearts really cannot be truly satisfied by anything other than the one who created them. Some years ago I memorised Job 22:24–26 (RSV):

If you lay gold in the dust,
    and gold of Ophir among the stones of the torrent bed,
and if the Almighty is your gold,
    and your precious silver;
 then you will delight yourself in the Almighty,
      and lift up your face to God.

For many of us, our deepest desires are like gold; they are precious to us, and because of that, we might hold them tight and close. And yet these verses seem to be encouraging us to lay down our gold, to allow the destiny of our gold to be beyond our control – a torrent bed is probably not the most stable environment for the preservation of gold! And further, we are encouraged to make the Almighty himself our gold, our precious silver; to make knowing and loving God our greatest desire, our greatest delight, our truest treasure. As we do this, we will discover a liberating truth – that we are free to delight ourselves in the Lord; free to lift up our faces to him with no fear or shame; free to own the desires of our hearts before a God who is the source of all desire, all delight, all fulfilment. And it may be that, eventually, with a full and free heart, we will be able to echo the psalmist's words when he declared, 'Whom have I in heaven but you? I desire you more than anything on earth.' (Psalm 73:25). May it be so.

A reflection: owning our desires

Some years ago, when I was struggling with a potentially life-changing decision that I needed to make, a wise friend tried to draw out of me what it was that I most desired. She explained that my decision would be shaped by that desire – but my problem was that I didn't clearly know what it was that I desired. My heart felt like the clothes table at the end of a church jumble sale: a tangle of mismatched dreams and hopes, an untidy heap of longings which seemed to have no clear shape.

Sensing my distressed confusion, she suggested I reflect on Jesus' encounter with Bartimaeus (Mark 10:46–52) as a way through my jumbled thoughts. I did, and it helped. As you read these words, you may not be struggling with an important decision, but there may be other areas in your life where recognising and owning your desires would be helpful in creating space for God to bring new life and growth to those areas.

The practice that follows is a classic way of reflecting on the word of God, where we picture the scene in our minds and then place ourselves intentionally into that scene as though we were actually there in person. It's actually a very natural way of engaging with a narrative. Whenever we read or hear a story, we automatically picture it in our minds, watching the actions and the interactions of the characters in our mind's eye. This way of reading God's word brings us naturally into the presence of Jesus and into prayer.

Practice: Praying with the gospels

- Choose a time and a place where you can relax without being anxious about the clock or about interruptions.
- Prepare for your reading by sitting comfortably but alert, and pray that the Lord would guide you in your reading.
- Read the passage as often as you need to until you are reasonably sure of its content, until you can picture it in your mind's eye:

Then they reached Jericho, and as Jesus and his disciples left town, a large crowd followed him. A blind beggar named Bartimaeus (son of Timaeus) was sitting beside the road. When Bartimaeus heard that Jesus of Nazareth was nearby, he began to shout, 'Jesus, Son of David, have mercy on me!' 'Be quiet!' many of the people yelled at him. But he only shouted louder, 'Son of David, have mercy on me!' When Jesus heard him, he stopped and said, 'Tell him to come here.' So they called the blind man. 'Cheer up,' they said. 'Come on, he's calling you!' Bartimaeus threw aside his coat, jumped up, and came to Jesus. 'What do you want me to do for you?' Jesus asked. 'My Rabbi,' the blind man said, 'I want to see!' And Jesus said to him, 'Go, for your faith has healed you.' Instantly the man could see, and he followed Jesus down the road.

MARK 10:46–52

- Now, place your Bible aside and picture yourself in the story, let yourself be in the place of Bartimaeus, but as yourself, with your own name. As you sit by the roadside, allow the setting to become as vivid as possible. You cannot see, but what can you hear, smell, feel?
- Allow the action to unfold just as it is told in Mark's account.
  - As Jesus approaches, what words do *you* call out to him? Are they the same words as Bartimaeus used, or are they different ones?
  - What are the voices that try to silence you? Do they come from outside of you or from within your own heart?
  - What is the 'cloak' that you need to throw off to come to Jesus? How do you feel about throwing it off?
  - Hear Jesus asking you that most important question, 'What do you want me to do for you?' What do you say in response?
  - What do you sense Jesus is saying in response to the desire you have expressed to him?

Allow this time of reflection to come to a natural end. Don't rush away from it. Take time to pray some more, to reflect and/or journal about what has happened as a way to capture your thoughts on this encounter with God and with your own desires.

5

A tale of
two yokes

'Come to me, all you who are weary and burdened, and I will give you rest. Take my yoke upon you and learn from me, for I am gentle and humble in heart, and you will find rest for your souls.'

MATTHEW 11:28–29 (NIV)

'Are you tired? Worn out? Burned out on religion? Come to me. Get away with me and you'll recover your life. I'll show you how to take a real rest. Walk with me and work with me – watch how I do it. Learn the unforced rhythms of grace. I won't lay anything heavy or ill-fitting on you. Keep company with me and you'll learn to live freely and lightly.'

MATTHEW 11:28–29 (MSG)

These familiar words of Jesus have touched so many of us. Weary and worn out, we have turned to them for comfort, for the hope of rest, for peace. Countless sermons have been preached on these verses, and many of us have books on our shelves with titles such as *The Resting Place, Working from a Place of Rest, Quiet Spaces*… all evidence of our hunger for answers to the questions, 'How can I experience the rest that Jesus is inviting me into when everything in my life conspires against that experience? What does this rest even look like?'

These are not newly minted questions for me. Over 20 years ago, I was discussing these verses with a dear friend who at that time had three children under the age of three. I was bouncing around ideas for a talk I was preparing on rest. Her response to my proposed content was a reality check for me; it was a memorable conversation that went roughly like this: 'If you are only going to talk about physical rest and the need to withdraw to somewhere quiet to get that rest, then you have nothing to say to my life and the reality of my days. Unless you can say something about rest that makes sense to those of us who are weary beyond words and for whom even one unrushed, demand-free hour alone would be a luxury, then I'm not sure that you have anything much to say.'

I rewrote my talk.

We don't have to be the mother of young children to resonate with the longing to experience the truth of Jesus' words soothing their way into the chaotic corners of our lives. We may be living with the constant demands of a job which pushes us to the tipping point of exhaustion; we may be in situations over which we have no control, situations from which there is no relief, and yet every day requires us to glean to the very edges of our love, our care and our courage, for the energy we need to get through that day. For many of us, the roles we fill, the responsibilities we shoulder and the emotional and mental and physical toll they take on us may make rest seem like an ideal for which we strive but realistically understand we'll never achieve. For many, life is an endless marathon which so often asks more of us than we think we could ever give and makes the very idea of rest a luxury we cannot afford to indulge.

In the years since that conversation I've studied and reflected and wondered about these verses so many times. I've tried to understand what these words would have meant, what their impact might have been on the hearts of those who heard them for the very first time – and also what they might mean for us who are separated from those first hearers by the stretch of centuries, but connected so closely by the common thread of our aching need for someone to come and tell us that we are seen and known, that our needs are legitimate, that our weariness is recognised and that there is hope of a better way to live.

The context of the invitation

As we saw in chapter 3, understanding the context of Jesus' words can enrich our encounter with them. As we understand something of how those first-century men and women might have heard those words, we might glean something helpful for our own lives today. A couple of chapters earlier, Matthew records that Jesus is deeply moved as he looks at the men and women who are crowded before him. He saw them as 'harassed and helpless, like sheep without a shepherd' (Matthew 9:36, NIV). The original words used by Matthew convey an image of fretfulness, of anxious lostness, of fear-filled vulnerability; the image is one of harried restlessness. And now Jesus was faced with yet another crowd; the faces may have been different, but their condition and their needs were the same. These weary ones needed to hear words which carried the power of compassionate wisdom about them, words which could ignite the hope of change, words which could birth new life. And Jesus brought all of this to them and more, as he invited these 'weary and burdened' ones to come to him.

So much can be lost in translation! We may think of being weary as being just very tired, but the specific word Jesus uses to describe the weariness of these men and women means 'weary to the point of exhaustion'. They were weary because they were 'burdened'. When I explored the meaning of this word in the original Greek, I was surprised to discover that the burdens these men and women carried had nothing to do with the everyday challenges of life in the workplace or the family, and everything to do with the demands placed on them by their religious lives.

The word translated as 'burdened' is rooted in the Greek word *phortizo* and conveys an image of a ship that has had so much freight put on its deck that it is in danger of listing and of losing both the cargo and the ship if just one more thing is added to it. It's the image of an animal so loaded down by what's been placed on its back that its knees are buckling and it is dangerously close to collapse. They are potent and poignant images – and as Jesus looks into the eyes and into the hearts of the men and women who listened to him that day, *this* is how he saw them, how he pictured them. They were God-fearing, sincere, hard-working men and women on the verge of collapse, overloaded, overwhelmed and exhausted. Jesus may have been the first rabbi they would ever have encountered who actually acknowledged the desperate reality of their lives – the sad truth that their religion was crushing the life out of them.

But how did they get to be that way? How did a faith that was meant to bring them fullness of life become so wearying, so exhausting, so life-threatening to them?

'The yoke of the Pharisees'

The short answer is that they lived under the yoke of the Pharisees. In literal, physical terms, a yoke was a wooden instrument placed across the shoulders of animals to help the farmer in his work. But in our Bibles, outside of this obvious, literal sense, the yoke is a metaphor for control and authority. The life of the ordinary Jewish man or woman was governed by the law of Moses, and in Matthew 23:2 Jesus tells us that the Pharisees were the official interpreters of that law. Not only that, but they had authority to uphold and enforce it. To be under the yoke of the Pharisees, therefore, was to be under their authoritative interpretation of the law, their particular understanding of how to live a life that pleased God. The Pharisees were specialists in the law of Moses, intent on making that law relevant for every situation that anyone could ever encounter. Driven by this intention, they had, over time, codified what was originally a very simply stated law into 365 prohibitions and 250 commandments, guaranteeing that every day became an exercise in futility, because there was no way that even the most sincere believer could keep this law. In Galatians 5:1 Paul describes it as a yoke of slavery, from which they would never, could ever, be free.

In their efforts to produce righteousness under the law, the Pharisees had reduced the wonder of an amazingly gracious and generously loving God to a nitpicking Dickensian bookkeeper of a God: a harsh, demanding taskmaster. As a result, the ordinary person's relationship with God had become all about doing for God, all about keeping God happy by trying to keep the law, by sacrificing to the point of hardship. It had become about getting it right, always.

These good and well-intentioned legalists had lost the forest for the trees. In their efforts to honour the law they had missed the expansiveness of the lawgiver's heart. They had lost the primary purpose of the law, which was to keep the people of God in a relationship with him in which they consistently experienced his love and care, his kindness, compassion and grace. Israel's purpose in the world was to be a witness to the wonder of belonging to this God; they were to be a living picture to the world of what being cared for, nurtured and provided for by their God looked like (Isaiah 43:10). They were to be like a light to the nations around them – illuminating the true character of this God by the way they lived their lives.

But the Pharisees had reduced all of this wonder into rules and regulations which allowed for no rest, no respite, and it was heartbreaking. There was no way that the people could fulfil the requirements of the laws that they had been given. It was a life sentence from which there was no reprieve, no parole; it was a crippling burden that never went away.

The yoke's on me

And it can be the same for us. We may not be living under the harsh dictates of the Mosaic law, but we may be living a particular interpretation of faith and discipleship which pushes us beyond anything which God may want for us. So much of how we live is shaped by our understanding of who God is, by the picture of God we may have built up in our minds over many years. Our days may be dominated by an internalised image of God as a demanding employer for whom nothing is ever enough, or a teacher who grades so harshly that we can never pass, no matter how hard we try. We can live under the burden of serving a God whom we believe is impossible to please, who holds a standard for our lives which we can never attain. No matter what we do, how hard we try or how many long nights and missed family occasions we offer on the altar of our service, it never seems to be enough. Some of us are working our hearts to the bone – but it still doesn't feel like enough to satisfy the insatiable need for more from the God we believe in. We might never articulate it so starkly, but in the hidden depths of our hearts we may have a growing fear that the demands of this God will eventually destroy our faith, our family, our very lives.

When I was a new believer, I attended the nearest church to my home. Every Sunday morning, the first thing I saw as I walked into the main meeting hall was a larger-than-life picture of Jesus painted on the back wall. Jesus held up nail-pierced hands, and above his head were the words, 'All this I have done for thee', and under his feet the words, 'What hast thou done for me?' Sunday by Sunday I looked at that image and read those words, and over time those words began to shape my understanding of how to live as a Christian. Somehow, I needed to repay Jesus; whatever it took, I needed to do it. But it became even sadder; over the next few years the joy and the freedom I had experienced when I first encountered the wonder of God's grace in Jesus began to be replaced by a legalistic understanding of discipleship that gradually dimmed the lights on grace and spotlighted effort and service. I came to believe that I would need to spend the rest of my life trying to be something and do something for Jesus which would justify his sacrifice for me. It was a never-ending demand, but one which I accepted as part of being a committed disciple of Jesus.

It's taken time and a different kind of effort to recover from the debilitating effects of those years, but I'm getting there. Unpacking this invitation of Jesus has been part of the journey as I learn to *come to* him before I ever *go for* him; to take from him before I give anything to anyone; to receive from Jesus what he wants to give me rather than trying to repay him for what he's done for me. It's been quite the journey, and it's an ongoing one, but a significant part of it has been acknowledging how very disappointed and tired I was by the life I was living. And I've discovered I'm not alone in this.

Many of us are tired of trying to live up to a standard we've adopted for ourselves or a standard we've adapted from the life of someone else – and it's not working. Many of us know what it is to live life as 'karaoke' Christians: constantly singing the cover version of someone else's life and wondering what it would take, what it would sound like, to sing our own song. So many of us are living a script that was written for us by someone else – partners, parents, teachers, bosses, pastors, friends. In our more honest moments, we may look at ourselves in the mirror and ask, 'What are you doing?! This is no way to live!' It's into *this* context that Jesus speaks his invitation words to those men and women in the crowd on that first-century day and to us on this 21st-century day as we read these words. Jesus is saying, 'Whatever the nature of the weight you are carrying, wherever you've picked up that burden, however long you've carried it, and however it's shaped your life – it's time now to come to me and to receive the rest I want to give you.' It's a very simple, straightforward invitation, but it's a profoundly challenging one too, because it demands that we be willing to radically reorder the priorities of our lives, that we be willing to live a life 'yoked' with him. Thankfully, Jesus tells us exactly how we can do that.

The yoke of Jesus

Verbs are important! There are three verbs in this invitation which signpost the way to rest. They are come, take and learn.

Come...

Come to me! Our English translations don't really do justice to the force of the original language here. When Jesus calls out, 'Come!', it's a strong appeal, a command. This is not a casual, take-it-or-leave-it invitation; it's an intense, heart-rending, earnest plea. Jesus *wants* us to come to him; he urges us to move away from our old ways of making life work and to move into a new way of allowing him to show us how to live. In inviting us to come to him, he is asking us to bring to him all that we are and everything that we are not; to come 'just as we are,' as the old hymn puts it. When Jesus says, 'Come *to me*', the 'me' is emphatic – it means 'come to me and only to me'. Jesus is basically saying to them, 'You need to know that you will not find rest in any other place except in me. You may go to other places, other people, other contexts to find your rest, but you will not find it in any other place but me.' Jesus claims that true rest, rest which brings us ease and refreshment, is found in him alone.

The specific rest that Jesus is referring to in this context is not primarily physical; it is 'rest for your *souls*'. The AMPC translation helpfully unpacks this phrase as: '[Relief and ease and refreshment and recreation and blessed quiet] for your souls.' Our souls are the deepest, innermost part of who we are, the place in which our truest self dwells, the place out of which we truly live, and it is in *this place*, this deepest inner self, that Jesus promises us rest.

In practice, it may be rest from the comparisons and competitiveness that dog our days: rest from lying awake at 3.00 am wondering whether we *are* enough or whether we are *doing* enough for our children, parents, friends and colleagues; rest from fretting over small slights, offences and grievances which bruise the tender places in our hearts. Soul rest is rest from the incessant demands of a perfect performance, from needing to achieve whatever it is that will give us the recognition and affirmation we crave to soothe the sharp-elbowed reminders of our inadequacy. What Jesus is offering us in this glorious invitation is not an escape route into an easy life, but an easy yoke, a way out of the stranglehold of a slowly suffocating soul. Soul rest is a steady restfulness experienced within the very demands of our lives, *in* the pressures, *in* the circumstances. It is not rest from working, but resting in the very midst of that work – or, as the title of Tony Horsfall's insightful book suggests, we work *from* a place of rest, not *to* a place of rest.[28]

Take...

In this invitation, as he invites us to take his yoke, Jesus is deliberately setting up a contrast with the yoke of the Pharisees. He is inviting us to live in an intimate relationship with him in which we accept and embrace *his* authority and *his* wisdom on how to live well. This is not an invitation to be yoked to a set of beliefs, a church or a leader, but to a real, living person who knows us and loves us and has our best interests at heart. It's an invitation to be drawn into doing life with him. Jesus is not asking us to give a single thing to him here in exchange for this rest; he is only asking us to take from him, to take the yoke of his authority on how to live a life that brings as much pleasure to the heart of God as it brings peace and satisfaction to our own hearts. He is inviting us to keep company with him and to allow him to lead us into a life which is characterised by the words 'freely and lightly'. I wonder if that's how we experience our life with Jesus – as free and light. It's hard to feel free and light when we constantly feel harried by our own needs or the needs of others, and hounded by the unrelenting hurriedness of our days, pushing the pace at which we live those lives beyond sustainable levels. The pace Jesus sets for us is so very different.

Pace

In the first century, the men and women around Jesus that day would have been used to seeing two oxen or other animals yoked together, pulling a simple plough or some logs or some other burden behind them. They would have known that a younger ox was always paired with a more experienced ox, and they would have understood that in order for it all to work, these two oxen would need to work together, walking at the same pace and in the same direction. The less experienced ox, yoked to the more experienced one, would soon discover that there was no way that he could go at his own pace; he had to go at the pace of the more experienced ox. He couldn't go faster, slower or in a different direction. He had to measure his rhythm to the rhythm of the other; he had to be sensitive to the pull of the yoke on his shoulders, to be attentive to the way the other turned, to the movements he made, to the breath he breathed.

And it's not too much different for us as we take on Jesus' yoke. Eugene Peterson, in *The Message*, articulates this movement so clearly as he unpacks the meaning of Jesus' words here: 'Walk with me and work with me – watch how I do it… Keep company with me.' As we are yoked with Jesus, we move into a way of living that is paced by Jesus. In the prologue to his gospel, John tells us that Jesus was full of grace (John 1:14); yoked with him, we are paced by grace, our lives shaped by a generous kindness. One of my favourite definitions of grace states that 'grace is nothing more or less than the face that love wears when it meets imperfection, weakness, failure, sin'.[29] His pacing of our lives is informed by his complete knowledge and understanding of us. Jesus knows us. There is nothing about us that he does not know. He knows the truth about our lives, he knows the reality of our days, he knows our dreams – and our nightmares. He knows what coaxes us into life and what crushes us to death. We are not paced by a disembodied app on our smart phones, but by a living person who is committed to our highest good, our deepest rest.

But we can be so easily yoked to other things – and we need to reognise that whatever we are yoked to will determine our pace, and our pace will in many ways, determine the peace and rest of our souls.

External pressures

We can be yoked to performance and perfectionism; we can be yoked to meeting the expectations of others; we can be yoked to a certain image of ourselves that we want to guard and protect because so much of our identity is wrapped around that image.

Living in an overwhelmingly high-tech culture, we can so easily be yoked to the world's perspectives of how to live our lives, to a relentlessly 24/7 view of life which demands that we be available to all people in all places at all times and for all things. Our smart phones only exacerbate that sense of constant availability; we can live bound by the anxiety and fear that turning off our phones or of not checking our emails at least once an hour will result in something awful happening – and it will be our fault... and so it goes on. When we equate care and commitment with availability, the only way to prove we care is to be available. It is such a warped view of commitment, and it pushes us beyond the limits of what is reasonable or possible for our lives.

I remember saying to a friend once, 'I can't seem to find the off-switch in my life!' You might identify with that and also with the fact that when you do find the off-switch and use it, someone else comes and switches it back on – in the shape of another demand, a request, an email, a phone call, a text – all of which ask us to go beyond what we know is wise and good, but which we may feel unable to refuse. Jesus spoke more than once about the cares of this world, the build-up of anxieties and pressures, the worry about the future and how we will live, and how these can ravage our peace and rob us of rest. He is not unaware of these pressures on our lives, or of the destructive effect they may have on us.

Internal pressures: destructive one-liners

But we can also be yoked to certain internalised one-liners – brief statements which have rooted themselves in our minds and which play automatically like well-worn tapes when we are in certain situations.

For those involved in paid ministry, perhaps, the shame-based phrase 'not enough' can be a toxic and explosive one-liner. We may feel that we haven't prayed enough, we aren't holy enough, we aren't wise enough, we haven't worked enough or we haven't given ourselves enough to people to justify our jobs, our income and the sacrifices people make to support us. But we don't have to be in paid ministry to feel the sting of this one-liner. Some of us come from homes where nothing we did was ever good enough; the standards that were set in our families meant that we failed more than we succeeded, so we lived with a constant sense of never being enough. Although we grew up, we never grew out of the controlling grip of that one-liner.

There are many other one-liners which may have made their way into our minds and hearts; we all have at least one which seems to dominate. For myself, a potent one has been, 'I mustn't let people down.' It has taken me years to work through the roots and the implications of this one-liner, because I found that it was such a strident voice in my life, a voice which yoked me to a treadmill of obligation and duty and which determined so much of my decision-making. I would find myself saying 'yes' to things I should never have agreed to – whether it was speaking somewhere, agreeing to mentor one more person, teaching an extra guest lecture at college or having a full summer of hosting guests in my little three-bed house.

My desire not to let anyone down has been a strong factor in my decision-making, but underneath it there was also a subtle desire to protect my reputation as a woman who was known as loving, caring and attentive to the needs of others, who was compassionate, wise and hospitable. In fact, I had become yoked to a distorted image of myself which I needed to maintain in order to feel satisfied with myself – and it was crippling my life. Learning to say 'no' has been a hard lesson for me – and it's one I'm still learning – but I am discovering that being wise and honest about my capacity and energy levels means that there are times when the most loving thing I can do for a person is to say 'no'. That one small word pushes me again and again into a dependence on Jesus for my reputation, but I'm discovering that it is also a doorway into a more wholehearted way of living, because when I now say 'yes' it is out of love and freedom and not out of self-protectiveness or fear.

Learn...

It seems that the rest that Jesus promises doesn't come from being staunchly independent but from being God-dependent. In Matthew 11:29 Jesus invites us to learn from him because he is meek and lowly in heart; he is humble. It's the word *tapeinos* in Greek and it describes the character of a person who is God-dependent not self-dependent, who willingly chooses God's way for their lives rather than demanding their own way.

It's a quality which is so evident in Jesus as he lived at the pace his Father set for him. We catch a glimpse of this in John 5:19, for example, where Jesus tells us that he only did what he saw the Father doing. Again, in John 12:50, he tells us that he only said the things he heard the Father saying. At the end of the first chapter of Mark, there is an insightful cameo which demonstrates how the truth of those statements worked out practically in Jesus' life: Mark 1:21–34 describes a full and busy sabbath day in Capernaum. Throughout that long day, Jesus has poured himself out for the needs of the people there: teaching, healing the sick in mind and body, delivering those who were held captive by various spirits. The next morning Mark tells us that 'Before daybreak... Jesus got up and went out to an isolated place to pray' (Mark 1:35), but some time later, his quiet space is invaded by the disciples, who inform him that all those who hadn't been healed by him the day before were now waiting for his return. They seem to be fully expecting a repeat performance of his miracles. But Jesus does the unexpected: he walks away! He walks away from the needs of people who would have had their lives transformed by an encounter with him; he walks away from the men and women whose lives could have been healed and restored with just a word or just a touch from him. How could he walk away from those needs? How could he just pack up his power and walk away? As I've reflected on this question over the years, I've wondered whether the most obvious answer is that something happened in the time that he spent alone with his Father that early morning. I believe that, given the tender heart of Jesus, only a word from his Father would have induced him to leave this particular set of needs unmet. But paced by the purposes of his Father, paced by the wisdom of his Father, Jesus walks away and doesn't look back. Jesus does not respond to the immediate need of the people gathered there, and he doesn't push beyond the pace set for him by his Father or by his own need to serve. He was the Messiah, but he didn't have a Messiah complex!

Jesus' example here teaches us that unless we take the time to withdraw, to step out of the rapid flow of our lives for some moments, we can be in danger of being paced by the needs around us and within us and not by the God who paces us with grace and wisdom. As we read the gospel accounts of Jesus' life, we can see that he seems to consistently take time out of an incredibly busy and full life to be alone with his Father. If we are going to keep pace with him, then we too will need to deliberately press the pause button on our busyness. We will need to intentionally structure our days so that there are unrushed moments to spend with Jesus. When we don't intentionally figure out a way to do this, even amid packed schedules, we may discover that our lives are not just busy but breathlessly hurried and harried.

We don't learn the 'unforced rhythms of grace' from anyone other than Jesus – and so, somehow, we really do have to make time and space for moments of connection with him which realign the skewed perspectives that our lives can spiral into when all that paces us is need. Even as I write these words, I can still see the intense frustration on my friend's face as she attempted to portray the reality of her life and how very hard it was to find those needed moments with Jesus while caring for three small children. But, amazingly, over time, she did find those moments – in early mornings and late nights and in the gift of napping children. Her rested soul – amid the rush of her days – bore testimony not only to the integrity of her desire for time with Jesus, but also to the refreshing grace which met that desire. And it can be the same for us as we respond to Jesus' invitation to come, to take, to learn from him the unforced rhythms of grace.

Closer to home

When Jesus looks at us, I wonder what he sees. I wonder if he sees the same kinds of people as he saw on that dusty road 2,000 years ago. I wonder if he sees men and women who are tired and weary and burned out in our efforts to please God, to care for people, to live a God-honouring life, to hold it all together. I wonder if he sees *us* as harassed and helpless because we have submitted to a yoke other than the one he offers – or whether he is delighted to see rested souls, living fully with vitality and energy because we are yoked to him. My guess is that he sees a mixture of both in any one person at any one time.

We may look at this invitation and the new way of living that Jesus is offering us through it and feel that it has an escapist, dream-like quality about it – but it's not a dream; it's how Jesus lived his life. This is the life that he invites us to share with him. It's a life which sings the song of a rested soul even in the midst of circumstances which would rob us of that song. It's a song which can transform our lives – and it's a song whose notes we can learn over time and with some practice.

Practice: Stopping

> Then Jesus said, 'Let's go off by ourselves to a quiet place and rest awhile.' He said this because there were so many people coming and going that Jesus and his apostles didn't even have time to eat. So they left by boat for a quiet place, where they could be alone.
> MARK 6:31–32

In these verses we see Jesus pacing the work of his disciples. In the middle of what seems to be an incredibly intense time of ministering to the needs of the people around them, Jesus deliberately withdraws his disciples from the situation. His intent is to take them to a place where they will be with him and where they can get some rest.

There are many notes which grace the song of rest. Some of these notes are spiritual practices which can ease us into a space where we can be most accessible to the restorative ministry of the Holy Spirit: practices such as sabbath-keeping, prayer, retreat, silence and the practice of the Daily Office can be really helpful. In the next few paragraphs, I want to sketch out a particularly helpful practice, the core of which I learnt from Tony Horsfall's book, *Working from a Place of Rest*. Horsfall calls it 'the discipline of stopping'.[30] It's a needful practice, especially for those of us who find it harder to hit the pause button on our lives. It's a way to follow both the example and the teaching of Jesus in stepping back from our lives for a while to rest and to recover strength and perspective for whatever may be up ahead.

Stopping: The purpose

Horsfall defines stopping as 'pausing for a few minutes or a few hours or a few days, to remember who I am, why I am here and to receive strength for the next part of the journey'.[31] In another book, appropriately called *Stopping*, David Kundtz suggests three types of stopping which give us the kind of breathing space that we need in order to do what Horsfall suggests. He writes about still-points, stopovers and grinding halts.[32]

Still points are those moments, pauses, intervals between activities and appointments, waiting points in our day, wherever they occur – in supermarket queues, at traffic lights, at the school gates – when we consciously stop, breathe, remember, if only for a moment, who we are; to consciously recall that, above any and every identity we could ever have, we are named as the one God loves; we are precious in his eyes and he loves us (Isaiah 43:4). It is a time to remember that our lives are not purposeless or random, but wrapped up in the glorious purposes of God; to be still, even for a moment, to gaze into the face of God and to see in that face kindness, wisdom, generosity, grace and love for all that we are – even now, even here. They may be fleeting moments, but they can hold an eternity of meaning as we consciously acknowledge that we are in the presence of the God who never leaves us and who is present *in* all things and *for* all things in our lives.

Stopovers are longer. A stopover may be an hour, a few hours, a day, a weekend, a week or more. And the aim during this time, according to Kundtz, is to do nothing – or, at least, nothing that would distract us from our purpose of being rested in body and soul. In reality, it is to do those things which bring us to life, which deeply nourish and refresh us. So what is it that brings you to life? What is it that nourishes your soul and your body? We might plan to read, nap, visit a place or a person who restores our soul, enjoy a meal, a good coffee – whatever it is that we know is restorative for us, this is the time to do it.

And then finally there are **grinding halts**, needed for those times of major transition, of change, of illness or bereavement: a time when decisions need to be made which are life-changing. These are not normally part of the rhythm of our lives, and more often than not they need whatever time it takes in order to work through whatever is needed. During such time, other responsibilities or commitments may need to be suspended for a while in order to honour the present need.

Stopping: The practice

While our grinding halts may not be so readily anticipated – they are often thrust on us by the force of circumstances – still points and stopovers can become part of the rhythm of our lives: daily, weekly, monthly.

Many of our still points just present themselves to us without any planning – the traffic lights turn red or the supermarket queue turns out to be a long wait because someone needs an item checked. In those moments we can stop and shift our focus for a moment. But they can be planned for, too. Brushing your teeth is a great still point, as is nursing the baby or waiting for the bus or the train on our regular commute into work. Our everyday activities can be baptised with grace as we take a moment to be still and to remember who God is, who we are and that our lives have real purpose.

- What are the regular activities in your day which hold the potential for being still points for you? You might want to choose a couple to focus on. Try them for a few days and, if they are not the best choice for now, choose alternatives.

Stopovers need more planning in order to be effective. As you look at your calendar, you might want to plan, for example, an hour a week, a couple of hours a month, a day or half a day every three months. Plan something good and refreshing in that time, something that you can look forward to, something that you know will be restorative for you.

I live on the edge of the Cotswolds, and every three months or so I take myself off for a morning to a lovely hotel in a nearby village. They have a small, beautifully furnished sitting room there, cosied by a log fire and quiet, because most people don't know it's there. This lovely room is open to non-residents, so I order a cafetière of coffee, settle into the chair nearest the fire, take out my journal and spend the next couple of hours going through what I have written over those months, underlining repeated words and phrases, highlighting scriptures or sentences which strike me. When I've done all of this, I put my journal aside and sit there, breathing in the fragrance of the burning logs and the quiet presence of God. In those moments, I open my heart to the one who always seems to meet me in that place. I lay before him all that he has brought to my attention, and I surrender them all to him, trusting that he will lead me in knowing what to do next. I so look forward to this time. Including the lovely drive there and back, it's probably only four hours in total, but it feels like a holiday for my soul – and my senses too, as I soak in the gentle beauty of the furnishings, the comfort of the chair, the crackle of the logs and the taste of good coffee.

- As you look at your calendar for the coming months, when are the times that you might be able to plan in an hour or more for a stopover? What would be refreshing and renewing for you to do in that time, something that you would look forward to?

Stopping, as a spiritual practice, is a way for us to respond to Jesus' lovely words of invitation to 'come with me by yourselves to a quiet place and get some rest' (Mark 6:31, NIV). Our still points and our stopovers give our worn and weary souls the chance to breathe, to be still enough to feel the cool breath of God on our hearts and our lives, to renew our energies for whatever lies ahead for us and to honour our creation in the image of God who himself stopped and rested at the end of that first creation week.

6

Make yourself at home

'Make yourselves at home with me... Make yourselves at home in my love... You are my friends.'
JOHN 15:7, 9, 14, (MSG)

There is nothing more important in life than learning to love and be loved.... Love speaks to the depths of our soul, where we yearn for release from isolation and long for the belonging that will assure us we are at last home.[33]

Home. At its best, home is the place where we take off our masks, put on our PJs and put up our feet. It's the place we look forward to coming back to at the end of a long day or a long journey. It's the place where we talk without fear, dream without limits and laugh with our mouths full. I wonder if this is how we experience our relationship with Jesus. This comfortable ease, this safest of all places for our souls? Jesus invites us to make our home in him, to make our home in his love – and out of that place to enjoy the freedom to live with abandon and joy; to live wholehearted, purposeful lives.

Location, location, location

Our final invitation is found in John 15:9, where Jesus draws his disciples into the heart of his love for them with the words, 'Remain in my love.' This invitation is a call to surrender ourselves into the longing love of Jesus and to make our home there. The Greek word translated 'remain' in many Bibles means abiding, dwelling, or being at home in a place. It carries the idea of permanence, of settling down into a place and staying there. Moments earlier Jesus had told his disciples to remain *in him*, to make their home *in him* (v. 4), and now he expands on that invitation – inviting them to make his love for them the place they call home. He is inviting them to settle down in his love, to allow the sturdy walls of his love to surround them and protect them, to keep them safe, to be the place out of which they engage with life.

In speaking of himself and his love in this way, Jesus was reflecting the nature of his Father's love. Centuries before, Moses declared, 'Lord, through all the generations you have been our home!' (Psalm 90:1). In Deuteronomy 33:27, Moses recorded God's words to the tribe of Benjamin: 'The eternal God is your refuge', or in the NCV, 'your place of safety'. Later, through the prophet Jeremiah, God had told his people, 'I have loved you, my people, with an everlasting love. With unfailing love I have drawn you to myself' (Jeremiah 31:3). *The Message* captures the meaning of this verse in a particularly vibrant way: '"Israel, out looking for a place to rest, met God out looking for them!" God told them, "I've never quit loving you and never will. Expect love, love, and more love!"' The home which God intended to be for his people was one in which they would experience a lavish and continuous outpouring of his love for them. David Benner writes that 'love is the welcome that tells us that this is where we truly belong, the assurance that we have found our place'[34] – and it is into *this place, this home, this love* that Jesus was inviting his disciples that evening.

At the Feast of Tabernacles, Jesus identified himself as the water which Isaiah prophesied would satisfy the thirst of all who came to drink from it (Isaiah 55:1). At the tomb of Lazarus, he identified himself as the God who brought life to the dead. Now, in the quietness of the upper room, Jesus identified himself as the eternal God who is home for all who come to him, a loving home for all who respond to his invitation. Jesus truly is the 'ideal home', the 'forever home' of our grandest dreams, and in him and in his love for us we will find our deepest sense of belonging, safety, security, purpose, identity, comfort, appreciation, affirmation, recognition – and so much more.

The glorious wonder of this invitation is that it comes at all! In our wildest dreams we could not make this up – that Jesus, knowing everything there is to know about us, still puts out the welcome mat, flings open the doors of his heart and, with a love that has been brewing since before time began, joyfully invites us to step in and make ourselves at home, really at home. Forever. Not sometime in the future – not 'home beyond the blue' – but now, here, today. Our home now and always is to be found in the love of the one who loved us to death, literally.

As a little girl in Sunday school, I learnt the simple chorus 'Jesus loves me, this I know, for the Bible tells me so.' There have been times over these last years when I have sung and sobbed my way through those brief lines – 'Yes, Jesus loves me; yes, Jesus loves me; yes, Jesus loves me.' When the deep waters of loss, of disappointed hopes and crushed expectations, of broken dreams and broken promises have almost swept away the courage to go on, these simple words have rafted me safely home again to his heart. Despite the circumstances, despite what those circumstances may seem to suggest about my life and about the character of God, *this* is truth: Jesus loves me.

In these final moments that Jesus had with his disciples in that upper room, he told *them* this truth – over and over again. He told them that they were loved. He knew what was coming. He knew that in a few hours from now, these men gathered around him so closely would abandon him; they would run into the night or deny him by firelight. Before the night was over, he would stand before his accusers un-befriended and undefended. He knew these men, and he knew that in the hours ahead they would feel bewildered, lost, grief-stricken, confused, doubting, fearful and hopeless. He knew that before everything that was to happen in the coming hours, they needed to hear that they were loved, that they would always be loved by him, that his love for them would never change – ever. This is the nature of his love. And so, he spoke his words of affirmation, his words of invitation.

We can picture the scene. They are coming to the end of their supper together; they will have sung the paschal hymns, eaten the bread and the lamb, drunk the wine. At this point in the evening, Judas has already left to betray him, and now Jesus opens his heart to the disciples who remain. As the lamps sputter and the shadows around the edges of the room deepen, into this quiet, this ordinary moment in this ordinary room, Jesus tells his disciples, 'Make yourselves at home in my love' (John 15:9, MSG). The love into which he is inviting them to make their home is no ordinary love; the very nature and character of this love is nothing less than the love he himself experiences in his relationship with his Father. His invitation in verse 9 is prefaced with the words, 'I have loved you *even as* the Father has loved me.' In this one sentence, Jesus is drawing his disciples, then and now, into the intimacy of the love between the Father and the Son. He is drawing us into the reality of his home life with the Father. The love which he himself experienced in his relationship with his Father is the paradigm for our understanding of his love for us.

Here is love...

Translators of the original Greek helpfully unpack the meaning and intent of Jesus' words for us here. From them we learn that what Jesus is saying is, 'Even as the Father has, does and will forever love me, I also love you.'

Those words tell us so much about the nature of the Father's love for his Son. They tell us that the Father has always loved the Son – a fact Jesus confirms later in his prayer to the Father, when he declares, 'You loved me even before the world began!' (John 17:24). Before there was ever a world, there was the Father's love for his Son; there was a time when there was no world, but there was never a time when Jesus was not loved by his Father. Every moment of Jesus' life seems to have been lived in the awareness of the reality of this love – the Father's love shaped his life, his every word, his every action. I believe that because Jesus was so soaked in his awareness of the Father's love, he was able to handle rejection, being misunderstood, misrepresented, slandered, betrayed, used and abused, without those things tearing him apart or causing him to withdraw or retaliate.

As we read through the gospels, we catch glimpses of this Father love which Jesus experienced even before he began his public ministry. On the day of Jesus' baptism by John, God the Father tore open the heavens to declare his love for his Son. At his baptism, as he stood dripping wet with water, Jesus was drenched once more – in a deluge of love and delight and pride: 'This is my dearly loved Son, who brings me great joy' (Matthew 3:17). Before he had done anything noteworthy to merit such delight or pride, Jesus was enveloped in the assurance of his Father's love, acceptance and approval. Later, he would tell his disciples that 'God the Father has given me the seal of his approval' (John 6:27). Jesus did not have to prove himself to God; he was already completely approved. There was nothing that Jesus needed to do to earn his Father's love; he was already loved and delighted in. These truths were the rock-solid foundations of his life.

Everything Jesus did seems to be rooted in his understanding of the depths of his Father's love for him. He tells his disciples that 'the Son… does only what he sees the Father doing… For the Father *loves* the Son and shows him everything he is doing' (John 5:19–20). When John writes about the love of God, he usually uses the Greek word *agape*, but here, the word that Jesus uses to describe his

Father's love for him is *phileo* – a word which means affectionate fondness, the kind of love which we find between good friends and between loving family members. Jesus knew that the Father was exceptionally fond of him. There is joy and delight in this love; the Father enjoyed his Son – and Jesus knew it. At the transfiguration, God the Father again affirms his passionate love for his Son, telling the disciples who were just waking up (literally!) to the wonder of Jesus, 'This is my beloved Son; listen to him' (Mark 9:7, ESV). The Father wanted everyone to listen to the words of his Son – because those words brought life to all who listened, and they reflected the heart of the Father – the creator and sustainer of all life. In these brief words, we hear the Father's affirmation of the worth, dignity and honour that was due to his Son. And Jesus heard those words too – and believed them to be true for him.

The Father's love was an affectionate love, and it was a generous love. Earlier in his ministry, Jesus had told the disciples that 'the Father loves his Son and has put everything into his hands' (John 3:35). Jesus knew that there was nothing that the Father withheld from him. All that the Son needed in order to live the life that his Father purposed for him was given to him. But there was even more! Jesus told his disciples that his father showed him *all* that he was *doing* (John 5:20). Jesus was given a front row seat in everything that his Father was doing in the world. There was nothing that the Father was doing that Jesus was not shown and included in. Centuries before, Moses had written, 'The Lord our God has secrets known to no one ' (Deuteronomy 29:29) – but Jesus knew them because his Father shared those secrets with him.

Jesus was also sure that whatever would happen, however hard things would get, there would never be a time in the future when he would not be loved by the Father. The words of his prayer in John 17 affirm his confidence that because of the Father's love for him, he would soon be coming home (v. 13), to the place that had always been home for him: the Father's heart (John 1:18).

Like Father, like Son

The Father's love for his Son was an extraordinary love, but on that night, Jesus wanted his disciples to realise that they too were loved with this same love. It was a love that would never change and never end. It was a love which was rooted in eternity past and which would stretch into all that was yet to come. It was a love which would lead Jesus to give everything for them – even his own life. They were his friends, and he would soon give his life to bring them home to the Father (John 15:13–15). Years ago, on the back of a matchbox I read a very profound statement: 'A friend is someone whose heart has become your home.' Jesus wanted his friends to be at home in his heart. He wanted his heart, his love, to be their home address.

In his classic book *Abiding in Christ*, Andrew Murray had this to say about how we could ever understand the love of Jesus for us:

> This love of God to His Son must serve, O my soul, as the glass [mirror] in which you are to learn how Jesus loves you. As one of His redeemed ones, you are His delight, and all His desire is to you, with the longing of a love which is stronger than death, and which many waters cannot quench. His heart yearns after you, seeking your fellowship and your love. Were it needed, He could die again to possess you. As the Father loved the Son, and could not live without Him, could not be God the blessed without Him – so Jesus loves you. His life is bound up in yours; you are to Him inexpressibly more indispensable and precious than you ever can know.[35]

These moving words remind us of our preciousness to Jesus, and because of that preciousness Jesus longs to bring us into the fullest experience of the Father's love; he wants us to know for ourselves that, just like he is, we too are loved and delighted in, desired and known by God the Father. Our lives have purpose and a place in this world where that purpose can be lived out. Just like Jesus, we are drawn into a relationship of honour, trust and joy. In his high priestly prayer Jesus confidently asserts, 'You love them *as much as* you love me' (John 17:23). In unwrapping this mind-boggling truth we discover that we are loved with as much affection and enjoyment and delight as Jesus experienced in his relationship with his Father.

Moments earlier Jesus had probably stunned his disciples with the words, 'for the Father himself *loves* you dearly' (John 16:27). Jesus is using the word *phileo* again, but here he is telling the disciples that the Father is exceptionally fond *of them*. The Father of Jesus is exceptionally fond of us! We may be so used to hearing that God loves us that we become immune to the wonder of the truth that God is genuinely, affectionately fond of us. I like to imagine that if he had a team, he would pick us first; if he held a party, we would be his first invite; if he had a secret, we would be the first to know. His face would light up when he saw us, his ears would prick up when he heard us, and when we did something – just for him – his grin would be eye-squeezingly wide! Fanciful perhaps, but as I read the parable of the prodigal son, I see such a Father: one who, with a complete lack of dignity, picks up his robe and runs down the lane, flinging his arms around the boy for whom he's been watching and waiting for so long, and one whose heart bursts with love and delight and generous grace when at least he brings this son of his love home. This is our Father's extravagant, exuberant love for us.

To know that we are so loved makes a difference in how we live because we thrive, we live wholeheartedly, when we know that we are loved. When we are in relationships where we know we are deeply and unconditionally loved, accepted and enjoyed for just who we are, without needing to be anyone else, we flourish. We live from the very best of who we are: courageous, generous, gracious and unselfconscious. We are able to face the harder realities of our lives with hope and confidence; we are able to handle difficult people with grace and difficult situations without fear. We can take risks and try new things – and if we fail, not feel like failures. We can make mistakes without feeling like our whole life is a mistake. We can accept our own weaknesses without berating ourselves and acknowledge the weaknesses of others without judgement. We do not have to be perfect to be accepted; we do not have to succeed to be a success.

We know something of who we are at our best when we experience such love – and Jesus knows it too. His desire for us is that we live permanently within the embrace of his never-ceasing, ever-present love for us. Paul captured something of that truth when he wrote that God 'had settled on us as the focus of his love '(Ephesians 1:4, MSG), which means that there is not a moment in our days when we are not loved by him, not a moment when we are not accepted, appreciated, delighted in, cared for, thought about, planned for and known by him. David knew this truth, and in a beautiful outpouring of wonder he sings, 'How precious are your thoughts about me, O God. They cannot be numbered! I can't even count them; they outnumber the grains of sand!' (Psalm 139:17–18). I remember many years ago saying to myself, 'One day, Jesus is going to wake up and realise who I am.' The truth is that he never sleeps, so he will never wake up! He has always known who I am – who you are – and knowing all there is to know, he solemnly says to each one of us, 'As the Father has loved me, I have loved you. Make yourselves at home in my love.'

A friend once shared with me a quote she had read by A.W. Tozer: 'He loves us for ourselves, and values our love more than galaxies of new-created worlds.'[36] My first response on hearing those words was that they could not be true – at least for me. Perhaps for others – but not for me. I could not believe that a perfect, holy, righteous God could love *me*, Mags Duggan, for who I was, in all the tumbling chaos of my heart, the tangle of my dreams and the masked insecurities and immaturities which I couldn't seem to shake off despite all my dogged attempts at obedience. Neither could I believe that he would, could, ever, value *my* love for him. How could that possibly be true? How could he ever value my sincere but threadbare efforts to love him? The cynic researcher in me needed more proof than the beautiful words of a well-respected preacher, so I asked the Lord to validate Tozer's words… and in the wonder of a grace which honoured the honest yearning under the bare-bold words of the request, he did just that.

Over many years, and with the careful building up of one scripture set on top of another, one irrefutable experience of love after another, the Lord built a towering testimony to the truth of his love – for me. Over time I began to trust that truth, and I began to live with it, began to anchor my life in the words of the many scriptures which testified to this love. When the awareness of my sin seemed to put a great distance between the Lord and myself, I would reach for the truth of Jeremiah 31:3, where the Lord affirmed that I was 'loved… with an everlasting love. With unfailing love *I have drawn you to myself*.' When I felt that my repeated failure to live as a disciple of Jesus would cause God to walk off and leave me to my own devices, I drew comfort from the writer of the book of Hebrews, who wrote that 'He [God] Himself has said, I will not in any way fail you *nor* give you up *nor* leave you without support. [I will] not, [I will] not, [I will] not in any degree leave you helpless *nor* forsake *nor* let [you] down (relax My hold on you)! [Assuredly not!]' (Hebrews 13:5, AMPC). When I felt like I would never measure up to my own potential, let alone grow up into the fullness of Christ, I declared to myself the truth of Zephaniah 3:17, which I had memorised in as many translations as I could find. I soaked my soul in the words, 'He will rest [in silent satisfaction] *and* in His love He will… make no mention [of past sins, or even recall them]' (AMPC), and the next words would always bring a smile to my heart: 'Is that a joyous choir I hear? No, it is the Lord himself exulting over you in happy song' (TLB).

God sings? Over me? What does he sing? He is love (1 John 4:19) – every action, every word is an expression of the love of his good heart – so the song he sings has to be a love song! Every love song that has ever been written is just the faintest echo of this love song that God our Father sings over us.

Slowly, slowly, over time, the hard-edged image I had of a notionally loving – but remote – God began to be transformed by these truths.

Like the development of a Polaroid photo, over the years a new image began to appear of a God who, unsurprisingly, looked just like Jesus. Jesus was clear that 'anyone who has seen me has seen *the Father*' (John 14:9).

Jesus reveals a Father who is generous and gracious, compassionate and kind; who is attentive to the needs of his children; who notices our fears and our tears and the breaking of our hearts. Through the many moments of his life, through his many encounters with so many people, Jesus unveils for us a God who is unfazed by our failure and faithful in the face of our fickleness, who confronts our chaos with his peace and whispers calm into our confusion. The letter to the Hebrews says that in Jesus we see the fullest, most complete and radiant expression of the Father (Hebrews 1:3). I looked and I saw. And he was lovely.

Since those early years, I have shared Tozer's quote and the scriptures that were so meaningful for me with many a discouraged disciple who, rather than seeing the love of the Father reflected in the face of Jesus, has instead seen a distorted image of the Father, often, sadly, in the face of some of Jesus' followers. Hebrews 12:1–2 encourages us to fix our eyes on Jesus. As we do that – as we fix our gaze upon the face that looks at us with such love, such joy, such deep compassion – we will see the face of the Father; we will know what it is to be loved to the core of who we are. And that changes everything.

Free love

That we are so loved is a stunning truth, and the wonder of being invited to make ourselves at home in that love, to nestle down into it, to remain in it, is equally stunning. But how do we do that? What does that look like in practice? Again, Jesus uses his experience of remaining in his Father's love as the model for our understanding of how to remain in his love. 'When you obey my commandments, you remain in my love, *just as* I obey my Father's commandments and remain in his love' (John 15:10).

To be honest, for some years, I felt uncomfortable with this verse. Cobbling together some very legalistic teaching and mixing it with my own experience of being loved, I had believed a half-baked truth that what Jesus was saying here was, 'You can earn my love by obeying me.' Or, on my more cynical days, 'In exchange for your obedience, I will give you my love.' It took me years to understand how this interpretation was such a travesty of Jesus' meaning here – but I don't think I'm alone in believing this interpretation. I think it's a narrative many of us have believed. James Bryan Smith writes, 'The narrative goes like this: Love and forgiveness are commodities that are exchanged for performance. God's love and acceptance and forgiveness must be merited by right living.'[37]

Believing this narrative, we conclude that when it comes down to it, nothing is free, especially not the love of God. If we are going to be loved by Jesus, we will have to earn it, probably by being a missionary, somewhere totally remote, alone, with no support and no internet connection. I recognise that this may be extreme, but I've spoken with many who believe that only the greatest sacrifice of our lives, our dreams and our desires, could ever satisfy the heart of God; that in order to prove that we are worthy of being so loved, we must imagine the worst of all possible lives, and then go and live them.

There *is* a cost to love – and Jesus paid it, in full. The obedience Jesus is talking about is not the necessary requirement for his loving us, but the natural response to our understanding of how thoroughly we are already loved. Obedience is not a requirement, but a response to the love, kindness, wisdom and grace that is poured into our lives, moment by moment by an inexhaustibly faithful God. When we divorce obedience from love, we are in danger of becoming frozen in legalism, substituting disciplined and rigid rule-keeping for the free surrender of our hearts in a relationship of love.

I was reminded of the nature of this responsive obedience a while ago when I came across Psalm 119:54 in an unfamiliar version, the 1996 NLT translation. In this version the psalmist writes, 'Your principles have been the music of my life throughout the years of my pilgrimage.' Music is to be sung and played and listened to – and danced to! As soon as I read this verse, my mind went back to a time when I was living as a language student in East Asia. Sometimes in the cool of a summer's evening, we would go on to the flat roof of our dormitory with a hefty cassette player (this was a long time ago!), and we would meet up there with our national friends – and dance. Our friends provided the dance music, and it was strictly two-step, three-step stuff – no disco or rock 'n' roll. I was taught 'The Chinese Three-Step' by a doctoral physics student, who seemed to have made it his mission to teach this foreigner to dance – and he did. After the first few clumsy moments some rules were established: I was not to look at my feet; I was to look at him; I was to keep one hand in his hand and my other hand on his shoulder; I should allow him to lead me; and I needed to relax. When I did this, the dance worked; when I didn't, toes were bruised and so were egos.

I learnt a great deal about practical obedience from those dancing lessons. I learnt that obedience invited responsiveness, not resist- ance. I learnt that my dancing partner knew the music and the dance moves far better than I did and that the better part of wisdom was to surrender to his leading. I learnt to keep my hand in his, to keep my eyes on his face and to move – quickly – when he moved me in a different direction or at a different speed. I've since talked with mountain climbers who have had similar experiences of responsive obedience as they've hung against rock faces, hundreds of feet above the safety of the ground below, and done exactly as they were told to do by the lead climber. They were told where to put their hands, where to place their feet and, as they listened and obeyed, they climbed that rock face safely and successfully. Resistance or stubborn independence in this place could result in death. Whether dancing or climbing, the core issue is one of trust. Can I trust the one who is giving me the instructions? Can I trust that he knows what he is doing, knows how to do it – and has my best interests at heart?

As I look at the life of Jesus, and at an obedience that led to death, I am convinced that it was the depth of his understanding of his Father's love for him, and the depth of trust which was earned by that love, which enabled him to embrace such radical obedience. Jesus seemed to know, in a bone-marrow way, that whatever the Father asked of him was governed by an unbelievable depth of love. Jesus' obedience to his Father was the overflow of his understanding and experience of that love; his whole life was a committed responsiveness to his Father's love.

I wonder if the lack of consistent joy and genuine excitement in living as a disciple of Jesus, if the yawning boredom which sometimes shrouds our lives, isn't actually rooted in our lack of fully understanding and embracing how deeply we are loved by Jesus and how transformative that love can be if we respond to it. Jesus invites us to make our home in his love, but we go house-hunting in other places – in the approval, applause and appreciation of others, in our successes, in our most important relationships, in all the places where we feel safe and secure, wanted and known. We may build up a following on Twitter, have hundreds of Facebook friends and be on first-name terms with people we consider important – but the truth is that none of this can ultimately satisfy our deep-seated ache for the love for which we were created. Nothing will ever satisfy our soul's deepest need for life in all its fullness as will accepting this invitation of Jesus to come home to him and to make ourselves at home, really at home, in his love.

The apostle Paul's profound understanding of this relationship between our experience of being loved by Christ and our experience of life in all its fullness is perhaps most clearly expressed in a triumphant paean of a prayer in his letter to the Ephesian church. You can almost hear the longing in his words as he tells them that he is praying for them to experience the fullest dimensions of Christ's love, not in an academic, theoretical way but 'to know [practically, through personal experience] the love of Christ which far surpasses [mere] knowledge [without experience], that you may be filled up [throughout your being] to all the fullness of God [so that you may have the richest experience of God's presence in your lives, completely filled and flooded with God Himself]' (Ephesians 3:19, AMP).

This prayer is words and music and a symphonic accompaniment for our better song! And it is ours to sing – whenever and forever. Even now. Even here.

Practice: Celtic circle prayers or Caim

Standing before the council in Athens, Paul, in unpacking the truth of the God he knew, stated, 'For in him we live and move and exist' (Acts 17:28). We may have read these words many times before. I myself had, but one day as I was reflecting on this phrase, I was struck by the thought that if God is love, my whole life is encircled by love. I live and move and have my being in love. In translating other words of Paul, J.B. Phillips writes, 'But now, through the blood of Christ, you who were once outside the pale are with us *inside the circle of God's love and purpose*' (Ephesians 2:13, JBP). Our whole lives are lived within the circle of God's love, a circle which will never be broken from the inside or breached by anything from the outside, a circle within which we are safe and free to move, live and grow.

Centuries ago, early Celtic Christians seemed to have grasped the significance of living within the encircling presence of God's love. One of their prayer expressions was the 'Caim' or encircling prayer. In practising this prayer, they would extend their right arm and, moving clockwise, draw a circle around themselves in the air. This circle represented the protective presence of God – his love and care for them – and they prayed from within this circle. It's a simple but profoundly helpful prayer form, which we might want to practise for ourselves. It's one I started practising many years ago after stumbling on a book of Celtic prayers in our college library.

Here are a couple of examples of prayers I often use for myself or for others:

> *Circle me, Lord,*
> *Keep peace within,*
> *Keep fear without.*

> *Circle [someone I know], Lord,*
> *Keep hope within,*
> *Keep dread without.*

> *Circle me, Lord.*

You might want to try this for yourself. Extending your right arm, draw a circle clockwise around yourself. If for some reason this is not physically possible in your situation, or you are not comfortable in doing this physically, then you can imagine this encircling of yourself or another person in your mind's eye. Then pray using this simple pattern, replacing the words and repeating the pattern as many times as you want to. It is such a simple form of prayer, but as I've used it for many years now, I've found that the gentle rhythm of the words and the thoughtful choice of those words bring a calm, a peace and a confidence to my heart and draw me into a deeper awareness of the love which is always and forever surrounding me, always drawing me home.

For ourselves:

> *Circle me, Lord,*
> *Keep [a life-giving quality] within,*
> *Keep [a life-diminishing effect] without.*

Repeat the prayer, substituting different words for the life-giving/life-diminishing words used. End the prayer with the simple words, 'Circle me, Lord.' And then be still for a few moments, allowing the echo of those words a place in our hearts.

For others:

> Circle [someone I know], Lord,
> Keep [a life-giving quality] within,
> Keep [a life-diminishing effect] without.

Again, repeat, substituting different words for the life-giving/life-diminishing words used, ending with, 'Circle her/him, Lord.'

This is not a complex prayer form, but as we take the time to choose our words, to picture the encircling love of God around ourselves or the ones we pray for, it can be profoundly transformative. Some years ago I composed a simple melody for the words of my prayer, and I sing it often in my times with the Lord, when I'm driving or when I'm walking. Many times in praying for others, I will picture their faces and sing this prayer over them, trusting that as I sing my song before God, his love will hold them and his Spirit will breathe life into them.

Epilogue

Sing to the Lord a new song.
PSALM 149:1

Many years ago, when I lived in Hong Kong, I would often walk past a beggar who wandered the streets in my neighbourhood. He literally had nothing; most days all he wore was a black plastic bin bag, held up by a piece of string wrapped around his waist. Clutching that bag with one hand, he would forage with his other hand for something to eat from the bins outside McDonalds or the other restaurants in the area. His sun-darkened skin was filthy, his hair and beard matted and tangled. Over time, I came to realise that although this man's body seemed whole, his mind was broken and fragmented; most days he would mutter incoherently to himself and occasionally fling a rude word or two at the passer-by who came too near his spot on the pavement. There were days when, before I even saw him, I would hear him, sobbing and groaning. I think those were the days when I longed to bring him home with me, to run him the deepest of baths, to feed him a good meal and to let him sleep, safe and warm in a clean bed. But I didn't.

Another person whom I saw regularly in my street was a frail-looking old lady. I have no idea how old she was, but her long and straggly grey hair and bird-thin arms and legs gave the impression of a life lived long and hard. She was no beggar; she was a hard worker who day by day stagger-jogged down the middle of the road, her back curved and bent under the weight of the small mountain of recycled cardboard she carried. She never seemed to look up or around and was oblivious to the sight of the luxury shops and the fancy cars which lined the street; she just kept her eyes to the ground, her feet to the tarmac. She just kept going. And again, there were days when I was literally moved to tears when I saw her; I would think of my own mum and how it would break my heart if she had to live the life this lady did. So many times, I wanted to lift the cardboard off her back for a while, sit her down in a nearby café and buy her an iced tea. But I didn't.

I didn't invite the homeless man into my home, and I held back on my offer of an iced tea and a rest to the old lady, because I was a young, single woman living far from home, with limited Cantonese, even more limited cultural understanding and good Chinese friends who advised me against such loving but culturally inappropriate invitations. I saw the needs and my heart ached to ease the burden of their lives, but I could do no more than pray and support those whose ministry focused on the neediness that lived there on the streets of Hong Kong. I couldn't get involved.

Jesus had no trouble at all in being inappropriately involved! He blasted his way through social and cultural conventions and through the walls of religious tradition to reach the hearts, souls and lives of the men and the women who sat, stood and carried their burdens along the streets of the towns and villages of Palestine in that first century. He spoke their language, he understood their lives and, owning the prophet Isaiah's words for himself, he declared on one momentous sabbath day in a synagogue in Capernaum:

> The Spirit of the Lord is upon me, because he hath anointed me to preach the gospel to the poor; he hath sent me to heal the brokenhearted, to preach deliverance to the captives, and recovering of sight to the blind, to set at liberty them that are bruised.
> LUKE 4:18 (KJV)

These hope-drenched words of Isaiah graphically framed the mission which undergirded, motivated and animated the invitations which

Jesus gave to the men and women who crowded around him, their desperation reaching for his hands – and finding his heart. In this mission statement, forged through the heat of the desert and Satan's temptations, Jesus declared that he had come for the beggared (the literal meaning of the word 'poor' in this verse), the broken-hearted, the bound, the blind and the bruised. Every single one of the invitations which Jesus gave was addressed to someone whose life was shaped by loss, by lack and by a profound awareness of need. His invitations to abundant life – to rest, to drink, to come home, to be free, to make desire known – were all offered to men and women who were *literally* beggared and broken by the circumstances of their lives; they were given to men and women who were bound and bruised by the crippling demands of both state and synagogue or by illness of body or mind; they were addressed to those whose eyes were physically blind.

When the children of Israel, exiled in Babylon, first heard Isaiah's words, they would also have understood them literally, as did those in Jesus' audiences. But they were also words for those who recognised that they were poor in spirit – aware of their desperate spiritual poverty; to those who were broken-hearted by the events of their lives and to those who were bound by legalism, bitterness, anger and fear. Jesus' words were addressed to men like the Pharisees, who in their love for the law had lost love in that law and were now blind to the very presence of love in their midst; men, whose zealous pursuit of holiness left them instead hollowed out, their hearts dry and desert-cracked, thirsting for the water that their suffocating dogmatism refused to acknowledge or accept as it came to them in Jesus.

The writer to the Hebrews declared that 'Jesus Christ is the same yesterday, today, and forever' (Hebrews 13:8). His understanding, his wisdom, his love and compassion, his power – none of these have ever changed. And the truth is that our needs have not changed either. When the layered skin of history has been peeled back, when culture has been scraped down to its bare bones, we discover that in the marrow of our being we are no different from the men and the women whose lives and bodies Jesus literally touched in those long-ago days. Now, here, today, *we* are the beggared, the broken, the bound, the bruised and the blind – every single one of us. None of us has a get-out-of-jail-free card for the harder realities of life, and how those realities impact our lives. And the amazing grace through it all is that the Jesus who entered into the chaos and the confusion, the barrenness and the boredom, the desperation and the desires of those men and women *then*, is the same Jesus who moves into our lives through exactly the same entry points *now*. And at the door of each entry point he holds out to us the most important, transformative invitation of all – the invitation to trust.

Over these past years of studying the invitations of Jesus and through the months of writing this book, one thing has become so clear, and that is that the common melody line, the leitmotif, weaving through each of the individual invitations which Jesus gave is this invitation to trust. An unspoken question lies within each invitation: 'Will you trust me?'

Will you trust that the life I want to give you is the richest, deepest, most satisfying life that you could ever live – and that I know how to give it to you?

Will you trust that I know every single thread of every single grave cloth that holds you bound and captive from experiencing the life I died to give you? And will you trust that I am able to break each and every thread of those cloths to enable you to live freely and openly?

Will you trust me with the thirsts of your life, your thirst for life, and believe that as you open those thirsts to me I will pour into the dried-up spaces of your heart the refreshing waters of my own life to saturate that heart, to flood your heart with life itself?

Will you trust me with your dreams and your desires? Will you trust me to hear the unspoken, inarticulate longings of your heart and to honour and respond to those longings with compassion, wisdom and loving power?

Will you trust me with the crowding demands of your days and the weariness that clouds your moments? And will you trust that, yoked with me, paced by my grace, my complete knowledge of you, my love and purpose for you, you will experience the deepest of all rests – the rest of your soul?

Will you trust that I love you? Will you trust that the reality of my unchanging, age-long love for you is the truest thing about your life? Will you trust that you are loved and wanted and that you matter to me – your life matters to me – and that my love for you is the home your heart has always yearned for? Will you trust me?

In these invitations, Jesus asks us to take a risk, to risk trusting him with our lives and how we live them. The following lines portray that trust, that risk, so vividly:

> 'Come to the edge,' Jesus said.
> 'No,' I said, 'I'm afraid.'
> 'Come to the edge,' he said.
> 'No,' I said, 'I'm afraid.'
> 'Come to the edge,' Jesus said.
> So I came to the edge, and he pushed me.
> And together, we flew.[38]

The invitations of Jesus call us to come and stand on the edge of our hopes, dreams, longings and desires. They call us to stand with him on the edge of our fears, doubts and questions, and to trust him to bring us into the fullness of life we have longed for and hardly dared believe possible.

A prayer of trust

As we end this journey together, perhaps we might imagine for a moment listening to that one question Jesus might yet want to ask us.

> Will you trust me, from this day on, to give you a better song to sing for the rest of your life? Will you trust me to sing the song of my love, my life, in you and through you and into a world that needs, so desperately, to hear it? And will you trust that this song will be enough to satisfy your longing for more, your thirst to thrive, your hope of a richer, deeper life than you've ever experienced?

As we learn this song, my prayer for myself and for each of us is that this song will carry us forward into whatever lies ahead for us with hope and courage, with compassion and fearlessness, with joy and an irrepressible thirst for life – and the energy to live it, which comes from the God who invites us to revel in the fullness of all that he is, all that he wants to be and all that he may yet be in us, and through us and for us.

> *Sing the song of your life in me, dear Jesus,*
> *Live the life of your love through me.*
> *Grace my days with the beauty of trust,*
> *My moments with the peace of your presence.*
> *And through it all, hold my heart and all it holds*
> *In the wisdom and the kindness of your own.*
> *Teach me my better song,*
> *And I will sing it, Lord.*
> *I will sing it for you.*
> *Amen*

Notes

1   Stephen W. Smith, *The Lazarus Life: Spiritual transformation for ordinary people* (David C. Cook, 2008), p. 19.

2   Richard Foster, *Celebration of Discipline* (Hodder & Stoughton, 2012), p. 3.

3   Anthony de Mello, *The Song of the Bird* (Image Books, 1984), p. 2.

4   Stephen W. Smith, *The Jesus Life: Eight ways to recover authentic spirituality* (David C. Cook, 2012), p. 72.

5   Dawna Markova, *I Will Not Die an Unlived Life: Reclaiming passion and purpose* (Conari Press, 2000), p. 1. Reprinted with permission.

6   Irenaeus, *Against Heresies*, Book 4, Chapter 34, Section 7. The original quote in Latin reads, 'For the glory of God is a living man; and the life of man consists in beholding God.' Over the years, the term 'fully alive' gradually came to be accepted as the meaning of 'living man'.

7   Composed in 1646–47, the Westminster Shorter Catechism consists of a summary of Christian doctrine in 107 questions and answers, written by the Westminster Assembly, a synod of English and Scottish theologians and laymen with the intent of bringing the Church of England into greater conformity with the Church of Scotland.

8   C.S. Lewis, *Mere Christianity* (Touchstone, 1996), p. 154.

9   Ruth Paxson, *Rivers of Living Water* (Moody Press, 1930), chapter 5.

10   Smith, *The Jesus Life* , p. 72.

11   Smith, *The Lazarus Life*, p. 122.

12   Smith, *The Lazarus Life*, p. 122.

13   Paula Rinehart, *Better Than My Dreams: Finding what you long for where you might not think to look* (Thomas Nelson, 2007), p. 24.

14   Henri J.M. Nouwen, *Life of the Beloved: Spiritual living in a secular world* (Crossroad, 1992), p. 21.

15   Quoted in *Cistercian Studies Quarterly*, Vol. 35.2, 2000, 'Atlas: reawakened memories and present-day reflections', Peter Gilmore, p. 237.

16 Brené Brown, *Dare to Lead: Brave work. Tough conversation. Whole hearts* (Vermilion, 2018), p. 126.

17 Brené Brown, *Daring Greatly: How the courage to be vulnerable transforms the way we live, love, parent, and lead* (Penguin 2012), p. 111.

18 John Ortberg, *Grace: An invitation to a way of life* (Zondervan, 2000), p. 11.

19 Chapter 8, 'Walking with the wounded', in my book, *God among the Ruins* (BRF, 2018), may be a helpful resource in knowing how to come alongside someone in compassionate and strengthening ways.

20 Dr and Mrs Howard Taylor, *Hudson Taylor's Spiritual Secret* (Hendrickson, 2008), p. 145.

21 Taylor and Taylor, *Hudson Taylor's Spiritual Secret*, p. 145.

22 Naomi Levy, *To Begin Again: Rebuilding your life after bad things have happened* (Thorsons, 1998), p. 52.

23 A.W. Tozer, *The Pursuit of God* (Tate, 2013), p. 21.

24 Philip Sheldrake, *Befriending Our Desires* (Liturgical Press, 2016), p. xi.

25 Sheldrake, *Befriending Our Desires*, p. xi.

26 Rinehart, *Better Than My Dreams*, p. 33.

27 C.S. Lewis, *The Weight of Glory and Other Addresses* (Zondervan, 2001), p. 27.

28 Tony Horsfall, *Working from a Place of Rest: Jesus and the key to sustaining ministry* (BRF, 2010).

29 Joseph R. Cooke, *Celebration of Grace: Living in freedom* (Zondervan, 1991), p. 13.

30 Horsfall, *Working from a Place of Rest*, p. 56.

31 Horsfall, *Working from a Place of Rest*, p. 60.

32 David Kundtz, *Stopping: How to be still when you have to keep going* (Conari Press, 1998), p. 53.

33 Smith, *The Lazarus Life*, p. 58.

34 David Benner, *Surrender to Love: Discovering the heart of Christian spirituality* (IVP, 2003), p. 13.

35 Andrew Murray, *Abiding in Christ* (CreateSpace Independent Publishing Platform, 2018), p. 79.

36 A.W. Tozer, *The Best of A.W. Tozer, Book 1* (Wing Spread Publisher, 2007), p. 123.

37 James Bryan Smith, *The Good and Beautiful God: Falling in love with the God Jesus knows* (Hodder & Stoughton, 2019), p. 77.

38 Stephen A. Seamands, *Ministry in the Image of God: The Trinitarian shape of Christian service* (IVP, 2005), p. 128.

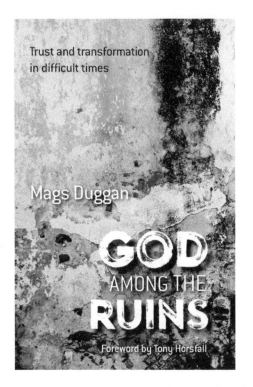

It takes courage to hope; to stand in our confusion and grief and still to believe that 'God is not helpless among the ruins'. Guided by Habakkuk and his prophetic landmarks, we are drawn on a reflective journey through the tangled landscape of bewildered faith, through places of wrestling and waiting, and on into the growth space of deepened trust and transformation. As you read, discover for yourself the value and practice of honest prayer, of surrender, of silence and listening, and of irrepressible hoping.

God among the Ruins
Trust and transformation in difficult times
Mags Duggan
978 0 85746 575 7 £8.99

brfonline.org.uk

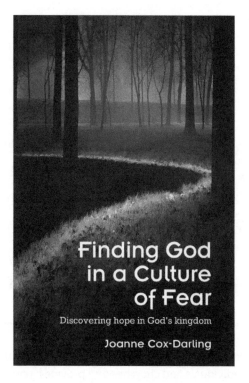

How can we live a little more hopefully each day? Fear, terrorism, corruption, fake news... it can be easy to become discouraged by the culture around us. Now more than ever, society needs hope in order to survive and flourish. This book takes us beyond comfort zones and easy answers, and towards a deeper understanding and practice of hope. It offers reflections, stories and practical ways for individuals and groups to find hope in their lives through discovering more about God in their midst.

Finding God in a Culture of Fear
Discovering hope in God's kingdom
Joanne Cox-Darling
978 0 85746 646 4 £8.99

brfonline.org.uk

Enabling all ages to grow in faith

Anna Chaplaincy
Barnabas in Schools
Holy Habits
Living Faith
Messy Church
Parenting for Faith

The Bible Reading Fellowship (BRF) is a Christian charity that resources individuals and churches and provides a professional education service to primary schools.

Our vision is to enable people of all ages to grow in faith and understanding of the Bible and to see more people equipped to exercise their gifts in leadership and ministry.

To find out more about our ministries and programmes, visit

brf.org.uk